CAREERS IN
TRUCKING

By
DONALD D. SCHAUER

The Rosen Publishing Group, Inc.
NEW YORK

Published in 1987, 1991, 1998 by The Rosen Publishing Group, Inc.
29 East 21st Street, New York, NY 10010

Revised Edition 1998

H.S. ⅟₀₀ 16.95

Library of Congress Cataloging-in-Publication Data

Schauer, Donald D.
    Careers in trucking.

    Includes index.
    Summary: Describes the opportunities, requirements, aptitudes,
and regulations involved in seeking a job in the trucking industry.
    1. Trucking—Vocational guidance—United States.
[1. Trucking—Vocational guidance.   2. Vocational guidance]
I. Title.
HE5623.S33   1987   388.3′24′02373   87-4769
ISBN 0-8239-2504-8

Manufactured in the United States of America

To Harold E. Clark, Jr.

Harold E. Clark, Jr., started his career as a trucking industry mechanic and held many of the positions covered in this book on his way to becoming a trucking company chief executive officer. He has long been involved in industry associations and efforts aimed at professionalism and industry improvement. His employees admire his frank and open nature and his willingness to discuss the serious issues facing the industry and the employees. Realizing that trucking is very much a people industry, Harold Clark has always given me ample opportunity to travel and meet with the people I was writing about as I prepared company publications. Without the knowledge gained from visits and interviews with the real people in the trucking industry, it would have been impossible for me to write this book.

Acknowledgments

The author wishes to express his appreciation to his many friends in the trucking industry, because it is their observations and assessments of their positions that are recorded in these pages.

Appreciation is also extended to the industry equipment suppliers who provided pictures of a number of the trucks in this book, to the Midstate and Fox Valley Technical Institutes for their curricula contributions, and to the American Trucking Associations for statistical contributions.

About the Author

Donald D. Schauer

Donald D. Schauer has served as director of governmental and public affairs for a midwest-based trucking company for more than ten years. During that time he has visited many schools throughout the midwest and southeast to talk with students about careers in the trucking industry. He has also served for three years on a public school system's board of education, and as a member of his Chamber of Commerce education liaison committee.

Schauer was a member of the American Trucking Associations Communications Advisory Committee and is a past chairperson of the Associations' Public Relations Council.

He is a graduate of Brown Institute and was in broadcast news before entering the trucking industry.

Contents

Introduction

Employing more than 7 million people and transporting 75 percent of the country's freight, the trucking industry plays a vital role in the economy of the United States and offers many outstanding career opportunities.

The trucking industry, which originated in the early 1900s and became prominent in the late 1920s and early 1930s, had a basic concept of placing a box on a truck and moving the box from the shipper to the receiver in the fastest, safest, and most cost-effective manner. This concept held true whether it was raw product moving to a factory, a partially finished product going to a finishing factory, or a finished product going from a factory to a warehouse or retail outlet. While this basic concept is still the only reason for its existence, the trucking industry has achieved a great deal of sophistication over the last eighty to ninety years. Today a wide variety of careers exist for those who enjoy the challenge of a people-oriented business with great demands for on-time schedules and service.

What the public thinks of as "trucking" actually takes many forms because the industry itself is highly segmented. Carriers are categorized according to those that haul other people's goods "for hire" and those that haul their own goods ("private carriers"). For-hire carriers range in size from the person who runs his or her own dump truck, to the corporation with truck fleets numbering in the hundreds or thousands that transport all types of raw materials or manufactured goods. Private carriers are usually manufacturers with their

1

own trucks to carry their own goods (so the words "not for hire" are painted on their trucks). Also, many companies use large trucks to provide services (for example, public utilities and construction companies) and may not be an official part of the trucking industry at all.

So diverse is the industry that its national trade group calls itself the American Trucking Associations (ATA). It includes subgroups that represent individual types of trucking and has state affiliates that deal with state-level legal and operational issues. The small local groups are highly specialized in their membership and concerns (for example, trash haulers and tow-truck operators).

Sophisticated maintenance and equipment-specifications practices, as well as computerized billing, rating, tracing, and dispatching, have opened the industry to a vast number of people with various skills and abilities, particularly in the data processing, network administration, and computer fields.

Management and demanding service times have resulted in operations positions for strategic planning experts, industrial engineers, and human resource experts who can motivate workers for maximum production.

Federal legislation in 1980 and 1995, which removed economic regulatory controls from trucking on the interstate and intrastate levels, respectively, has redefined sales and marketing in the trucking industry. Today, 100,000 or more trucking companies compete for a finite amount of freight, which does not increase with the increase in the number of companies competing for it. The industry's marketing and sales needs today present a tremendous challenge for an innovative young person motivated for success.

Another area of trucking that has undergone substantial change in recent years is the field of maintenance and equipment specifications. Equipment design

2

and maintenance has been revolutionary, as companies seek ways to increase fuel efficiency, prolong the life expectancy of equipment, and enhance equipment productivity.

This book will help young people considering a career in trucking become aware of the many options the industry offers. It will explain the challenges of the industry and the pros and cons of the various positions available. The qualifications for those positions and the personality types most apt to be successful in them are also covered. You will learn about the experiences of actual people who are already in trucking. Finally, this book offers several suggestions that might help a young person find that first job in trucking.

1

The History of the Trucking Industry

The trucking industry and its employees enable residents of Wyoming and Ohio to enjoy fresh oranges from Florida; computers on Wall Street in New York to run on software from the Silicon Valley in California; and automakers in Detroit, Michigan, to equip their new cars and trucks with parts from all over the country. Trucks that transport parts to assembly lines and warehouses are scheduled so close to production and order fulfillment that the parts are moved directly from the trucks to the production line. This eliminates the costs of inventories, warehousing, and rehandling, which result in production reductions. This just-in-time delivery concept helps U.S. automakers and other manufacturers keep pace with foreign competition, and it also increases the importance of trucking to our economy.

However, before we can further discuss the field of trucking, a knowledge of its history is extremely important in understanding how it operates. It can also provide a clue to the future of the industry.

Many of the large trucking companies operating today got their starts some seventy years ago, but they did not start big. Most of them began as family companies with one or two trucks. In some cases, a husband operated and maintained the truck while his wife handled the bookkeeping and business end. In other instances it was a father and one or more sons who operated the business.

The company I am most familiar with started almost sixty years ago when two brothers began hauling paper for some Wisconsin mills that had been using train transportation to move their products to Chicago Illinois. The Wisconsin paper mills knew they had a superior product; however, they were losing customers to Michigan mills that used truck transportation and got their shipments to Chicago faster. The Wisconsin mills soon realized the importance of service, and the two brothers were kept busy moving the shipments of paper to Chicago and bringing back other products that were sold by area retailers or used in the papermaking process.

The brothers were concentrating only on making a living for their families and had no plans of expanding the business in those early days. However, the paper mills' needs to meet demands for service soon made growth necessary. A third truck was added, and a driver was hired to operate it; the trend continued until a small family business became a large company.

What happened to the trucking company in Wisconsin occurred in many other trucking companies around the country. They were established to meet the service needs of one industry, and then kept growing and handling other types of freight, until they became full-service common carriers.

In those early days of trucking, employees generally worked long hours with pride and a desire to be an important part of the nation's growth. A driver might drive the truck all night and then spend a good part of the next day servicing it to be ready for the next night's load. Even some of the office workers occasionally took a turn behind the wheel of a truck at night if the company needed them.

Long hours and hard work were not unique to the trucking industry. In those days, most industries in the United States had similar working conditions. However, those conditions made the trucking industry as susceptible to unionization as many of the other heavy industries. Productivity in the industry did not necessarily increase with the better wages and improved working conditions brought by unionization.

During this period an event occurred that was of historic importance to the trucking industry. On August 9, 1935, the Motor Carrier Act was signed into law by President Franklin D. Roosevelt, bringing a large degree of stabilization to what was an often unstable and chaotic industry. Until then, trucking companies had been free to send their trucks wherever they chose, to compete for the most lucrative routes to the larger communities, and to provide no service at all to the less lucrative runs. Under the act, the Interstate Commerce Commission was empowered to regulate the industry. The Commission granted operating authority only when a need for more freight-moving capacity could be proved by the carrier seeking authority. All companies serving a particular lane had to charge the same rates, and the industry was required to provide equal service to large and small shippers and to large and small cities.

For more than forty years the trucking industry was regulated by the government this way. The regulation was probably a major factor in the development of many of the industries that started small in rural America. It was probably also the only chance for survival for many smaller communities that had no rail service at all. These communities had to rely on trucks for all goods brought in and for shipment of all the goods they manufactured or grew.

Economic regulation was also a major factor in the development of the trucking industry itself, which grew into what some consider the best transportation system in the world. Under regulation, a carrier could develop and grow without fear of a cut-rate competitor coming in and putting it out of business. Although entry into the industry or to a new area of service required substantial proof of shipper need as well as shipper support, new companies did enter the industry during economic regulation. Once in business, however, the new carrier had to operate by the same rules and rates as the carriers already established in that area.

Many observers argued, however, that economic regulation hampered competitive pricing. Congress passed the Motor Carrier Act of 1980, designed to open up the industry. It was called truck deregulation, although a substantial amount of regulation still existed. The legislation made it possible for anyone to start a trucking company and for existing companies to expand their operating areas. Most established companies opted for forty-eight-state operating authority.

All this activity resulted in much overcapacity, and, as in any other industry, when a surplus exists the price of the product or service decreases.

Before deregulation, the trucking industry on average earned only about a nickel on every dollar of sales. Deregulation and overcapacity soon resulted in rate-cutting and discounts of up to 50 percent. New non-union companies with lower labor costs were able to flourish in this competitive climate, while a number of established carriers with fixed overhead and union contracts soon found that competing in that climate ultimately led to bankruptcy. Many went out of business.

It is important to note, however, that not all of the established companies became casualties of deregulation. Many, in fact, flourished and became stronger. They did so by greatly increasing their volume and eliminating any waste that might have existed from the regulated era. They also found that not all shippers demanded the 50 percent discounts. Many shippers today insist on excellent service and realize it will disappear if too much price pressure is exerted. As a result, some of the cut-rate companies have perished as they found that low rates alone could not build a successful trucking business.

While the competitive nature of the industry continues, there are signs that more sophisticated truckers and shipping departments are producing a slightly less unstable atmosphere.

Young people seeking careers in trucking must be aware of the competitive climate and the performance demands that will face them. The carriers that will be successful in the future will be those with a conscientious team of employees, who will go the extra mile to assure the customer of the best possible service.

2

Truck Driving

Many people have a romanticized notion of what a career in trucking involves. Some young people are drawn into becoming truck drivers by the image of free-spirited individuals moving across the country, being their own boss, setting their own pace, without a care in the world, and in some cases feeling above the law in large, powerful, fast-moving vehicles. Be assured, though, that while this picture of a truck driver may be romantic, it is also very unrealistic.

A more realistic picture would be of a hard-working individual spending a great deal of time away from family and home, operating under unpredictable weather conditions, and always trying to meet a schedule. Often the driving is done at night and sleeping occurs during the daytime hours. Not very glamorous. But it is also a picture of an individual who in most cases loves what he or she is doing, knows how important it is to the nation's economy, and enjoys a paycheck that can exceed what he or she could make in another career.

THE OVER-THE-ROAD DRIVER

There are, in fact, a number of categories of drivers. The first one we will look at is the over-the-road driver. In the past, this driver was referred to as the long-haul driver. This driver is employed by a company and drives company-owned equipment.

The over-the-road company driver is among the highest paid; however, one must consider more than salary before making a commitment to such a career. Obviously, enjoying this type of work is essential. Also important is being the type of person who can adjust to the lifestyle often needed to be successful in this field.

You may be fortunate enough to have a job in which you take a load to a city about four or five hours away and are home by morning with a return load. If you work for a larger company, however, you might have to drive eight to ten hours, sleep in a motel or driver dormitory, and pick up another load that takes you even farther from home. It is not uncommon for a driver to leave home on Sunday evening and not return until Saturday morning.

Although young people considering such a career might not have a spouse and children when they start out in the business, most of them will want to settle down someday. Once a family is involved, there will be birthdays, anniversaries, school plays, music recitals, and other special events missed by the trucking parent. With the right attitude and the right spouse, all of these hurdles can be dealt with. It is important, however, to consider this aspect of the lifestyle before considering a career as an over-the-road trucker.

It is also important to note that truck driving is no longer exclusively a man's job. Women are entering the industry as over-the-road truckers, and truck-driving schools are getting an increasing number of women applicants. However, women with children should realize that a career in trucking may mean spending a lot of time away from home. It can be very hard to leave children at home to go on a long trip. The women you do find in trucking are often those who have opted not to have children, or who have already raised their children.

There are also husband-and-wife teams. Team drivers generally work for companies that truck cross-country. One member drives while the other sleeps. It is almost certain that as women seek careers with greater earning potential, more of them will become professional over-the-road truckers.

Karrie: Driver-Mom

Karrie is in her thirties, divorced, and the mother of two young children. When Karrie is in a rig she is her own boss, and she enjoys having control of her life and the satisfaction she gets from being behind the wheel.

Karrie's children do affect her career decision. She has made several employment changes so she could be with her children on a more regular basis. Her first job kept her away from home for several weeks at a time. While she was trucking, her children were at their grandmother's house. That arrangement worked quite well, but Karrie found she wanted more time with the children, so she quit that job. Her second job assured her that she would get home each weekend, but she soon found that was not enough time with her children, so another job change was made.

Today, Karrie is still an over-the-road driver, but she generally accepts only trips that get her home every night. This arrangement helps with her family goals, but it also cuts down on the amount of money she can earn. However, Karrie still finds trucking more lucrative than the secretarial positions she held before entering the trucking industry. Her only regret is that she didn't get into trucking sooner.

A License to Drive

Today, every person in the country who wants to drive a truck must obtain and hold a special license known as a Commercial Driver's License (CDL).

11

Prior to federal legislation that was passed in the late 1980s, each state issued its own licenses to truck drivers. The major problem was, however, that many states did not do much to determine how qualified the holder was to operate a large truck. Standards varied from state to state and some had no standards at all.

Another problem was multiple state licenses, which made it possible for reckless drivers to get traffic tickets in various states on different licenses and avoid the loss of driving privileges that would have resulted with a single license.

All fifty states and the District of Columbia now issue a CDL based on federal guidelines. The written and driving tests cover the same material, though some states are tougher than others in the amount of knowledge and detail they demand. However, even states that were lax are now fairly stringent. The larger the truck to be driven, the higher the skill levels demanded and the more "endorsements" the prospective driver must earn through studying and testing.

A driver is limited to only one CDL, and a centralized computer system keeps track of the license and driver to try to prevent the old multiple license problem. Some drivers who had been in the business for a long time resisted implementation of the CDL program in the early 1990s. They retired rather than study for the sometimes difficult tests. This contributed somewhat to an existing shortage of over-the-road drivers.

Driver Shortage

But there are more serious causes for the chronic shortage: The economy has remained healthy for years, meaning a lot of freight has to be moved by a lot of trucks. Many motor carriers constantly expand their fleets, requiring more drivers. Drivers find the job includes long hours, tough working conditions, and

Modern truck-tractor pulling a 48- or 53-foot-long van trailer is a common sight on today's streets and highways. The tractor usually has aerodynamic styling to reduce wind drag and improve fuel efficiency.

days and weeks away from home, family, and friends. They discover that the work isn't as fun as they had hoped, so many quit and go into some other career. Those who stay tend to change jobs, going from one trucking company to another in hopes of finding better pay or working conditions.

The driver shortage is estimated at between 500,000 and 1 million. In fact, the health of the economy dictates how many drivers are needed at any given time. One of the more respected organizations involved in the education of future drivers predicts that the industry will need about 450,000 more new drivers annually for a number of years. Because the economy operates on supply and demand, the salaries of future truckers

13

could well be determined by the extent of the driver shortage.

Age and Experience

Young people desiring a career in trucking face a number of frustrations. One of those frustrations is an age requirement, that a driver be at least twenty-one, set by the U.S. Department of Transportation. A majority of companies employing over-the-road drivers require that they be even older; some specify twenty-five years of age. Driving experience and a good work record are a plus, but that in itself is a difficult challenge for a prospective trucker: Everyone is looking to gain experience, but who will hire you so that you can get that experience?

Excellent experience can be gained in many local trucking positions that do not have the age requirement. Such a position might be found with a business that does hauling from one plant to another in the same city. Department of Transportation age requirements usually do not apply to that type of trucking. Driving a truck for a farmer may not be as exciting as a cross-country trucking job, but it would look good on a résumé, especially when accompanied by a letter of recommendation and an excellent driving record.

A good truck-driving school can be helpful, but you need to be cautious, as some schools make exaggerated employment claims. Getting a job is sometimes dependent on the health of the economy. When the economy is slow, the need for truck drivers is always down. There are some good private schools and a number of state-supported vocational technical schools that offer driver courses.

The Professional Truck Driver Institute of America (PTDIA), an organization that evaluates truck-driving schools, is recognized by many in the industry. If a

Driving a local delivery truck for a food or beverage distributor or manufacturer can be a career in itself, or it can lead to other opportunities in the trucking industry.

truck-driving school earns PTDIA accreditation, it probably has a legitimate program. Listed in the back of this book are schools from various states that have been approved by PTDIA.

The cost of attending truck-driving schools can vary greatly. The state-supported vocational schools are generally the least expensive. Some of the private schools have tuition charges that run up to $5,000.

In the past, most companies did not require driver-school training, preferring actual experience. With the CDL requirement and the industry-wide driver shortage, driving schools are gaining popularity. Some of the larger trucking companies may even have a joint program with a truck-driving school. The basics of driving may be taught by the school, while specific operating procedures and company safety policies are taught by the company in an extended program. It is advisable to check with a prospective employer before spending money on a school. The company may have a preferred school or course of study.

If you opt to attend a driving school rather than obtain on-the-job training, be sure that the school you select will help you reach your ultimate goal. Appendix I of this book contains a listing of the Proposed Minimum Standards for Training of Tractor-Trailer Drivers published by the Federal Highway Administration's Office of Motor Carriers.

It Takes a Professional

Trucking companies today are looking for people who will not only be truck drivers, but professional truck drivers. Thus, the résumé of a good prospective over-the-road trucker would include a high school diploma, some experience as a truck driver, a CDL, a safe driving record, and a good recommendation from a previous employer. Your home life should also be stable enough to withstand the occasional long absences without seriously hurting the quality of family life. You will be required to remain drug- and alcohol-free while working, and take a pre-employment drug test and possibly random tests throughout your career.

In most cases you will be asked to complete a job application form when you submit your résumé. Copies of letters of recommendation from previous employers could be submitted at this time. You should be prepared to supply accurate background information, including education, work experience, and names and addresses of former employers and those you can list as references. If you know someone already working for the company who is a good employee, you may want to list

16

his or her name also. Even more important, if you are known or well liked by a customer of the trucking firm, be sure to list that customer as a reference.

When visiting a trucking company to apply for a job as a trucker, you might need to see various people, depending on the type of company and the nature of its business. If you are seeking employment with a major carrier that has terminals in many cities, you may want to talk to the local terminal manager or the operations manager, depending on the size of the terminal. For a job with a manufacturing company that has its own fleet of trucks, you may need to meet with the director of transportation or the fleet safety director. If your application is with a trucking firm's home office, you may need to meet with the director of personnel. In any case, the receptionist can generally direct you to the right person.

When you go to apply, you should be well dressed and well groomed. Good, clean, well-maintained casual clothes are appropriate.

Trucking is a career that does not necessarily have geographical limitations. Probably at least one trucker lives in every little town in the country, including those so small they only have a post office and a general store. Obviously, the larger the city, the more jobs there are. But virtually every region of the country has a working economy because of truck transportation, and that means truck drivers.

Your salary as an over-the-road truck driver could vary greatly depending on what type of company you work for. Most over-the-road drivers are paid by the mile, so your annual salary would depend on the number of miles you drove. There is also a variation in pay per mile.

Drivers who work for a company with a Teamsters union contract are among the best paid. A union is an

Local and regional operations involve "daycab" tractors pulling a wide variety of trailers. These drivers get home often, sometimes every night.

organization workers join with the purpose of receiving better pay and better working conditions through negotiating with employers as a group. The Teamsters union represents truck drivers. Through collective bargaining, companies and the union agree to a contract. This contract allows drivers to earn more, although nonunion carriers offer competitive driver salaries. Some union drivers with enough seniority to get the trips they want have annual salaries up to and exceeding $50,000.

You should know, however, that most of the new trucking companies in the industry are now nonunion. The job availability will probably be greater with these new companies. Their drivers may not reach the $50,000 figure, but a salary of between $25,000 and $40,000 is possible for the hard-working driver who

18

gets in as many miles as he or she can legally drive. Wages for over-the-road drivers have climbed in recent years because companies have grown tired of trying to hire drivers away from rivals or spending large amounts of money training novices who soon quit for better-paying jobs elsewhere.

OWNING YOUR RIG

Owner-operators are truckers who own their own tractor (front of the truck with the engine), and sometimes trailer (back of the truck where shipments are stored), depending on the arrangement they have with the company with which they contract.

In most cases owner-operators lease their equipment to a company that provides them with loads of freight. They are paid a percentage of the revenue generated for the shipment of that load. There are many types of owner-operator contracts, however. In some cases they are paid by the mile, or they may even secure their own loads and keep all of the revenue generated by the shipment. Whatever the arrangement, they are sure to have additional responsibilities that a company driver does not have to worry about.

The company drivers collect their pay after the job is done and, for the most part, keep all the money for their own use. The owner-operators, on the other hand, have to pay for fuel, oil, tires, repairs, and make payments on their equipment. Whatever remains they get to keep for their labor, but if they are not careful there may be very little left. It is vital that they know their equipment and fuel costs before they accept a load. Rates vary for almost every load, and because of the competitive nature of the industry, some loads actually cost the owner-operator to haul them because they do not generate enough revenue to cover expenses. Many owner-operators have gone out of business because of this. On

19

Owner-operators and small fleets often buy traditionally styled tractors with lots of chrome and stainless steel trim, dual exhaust stacks, and powerful engines. They like the look and feel of such equipment, even if it carries a premium price.

the other hand, some have done quite well for themselves and their families. Still others have developed their one-truck operation into a trucking company and employ a number of drivers to operate their fleet. Let's look at two examples.

Rick

Rick is a young man with a wife and three young children. Rick wanted to be a trucker, and with the help of his father he secured the financing to purchase a rig after his twenty-first birthday. Financing was not the only benefit Rick's father provided. An accountant, Rick's father set him up with a bookkeeping system that lets Rick know exactly how much revenue a load must generate to cover the cost of equipment, repairs, and fuel, and still provide income for his family. Rick makes sure that the loads he takes generate the necessary revenue. He also knows that he has to keep rolling, because the fixed costs for equipment are there whether he is hauling freight or standing still.

Ed

Ed is a middle-aged man who made a living as a dairy farmer before he gave trucking a try. As a result of a divorce, Ed turned the dairy farm over to his grown children and purchased his first truck. Having learned hard work on the farm as well as obtaining some business experience with the dairy operation, Ed was set for success. He loved work, kept his rig loaded and rolling, and soon found the owner-operator business so profitable that he purchased a second rig and then a third and hired more drivers. Most recently, Ed had four rigs on the road and was finding business very lucrative. He attributes his success to hard work and a business approach to trucking.

This is not to say that those who do not succeed are not hard workers or good business people. Being an owner-operator is a business with a potential for success or failure just like any other business. During times when the economy is weak, there sometimes aren't enough good loads to make it possible for owner-operators to pay for their equipment.

With the risks that exist in the owner-operator trucking business, why would anyone buy a rig rather than go to work as a company driver? There are a number of good reasons. One of the biggest is the desire for

Specialized freight needs specialized equipment, like this "dropdeck" flatbed trailer which can carry tall loads.

independence and the satisfaction of having a business of your own. It is also possible that no company driver positions are available, a situation that seldom exists for an owner-operator. If you have your own rig, you can almost always find someone who will contract for your services.

As is the case with company drivers, owner-operators really do not have any geographical limitations. A visit to almost any truckstop will find a bulletin board covered with calls for owner-operators. These are usually offered by "brokers" who sit in a small office, using a telephone or computer link-up to find loads of freight through their contacts with shippers, who are searching for owner-operators to haul them.

The revenue paid varies greatly with the load; revenue is influenced by the type of commodity (some are more valuable and therefore pay more to haul), how much is being moved out of a given area at a given time (the more goods, the higher the revenues), and how many trucks are available to provide transportation (the fewer the trucks, the higher the revenue).

However, the majority of owner-operators contract with established carriers who keep them busy by assigning them to loads. These contracts also vary in how much they pay and how many of the trucker's expenses will be reimbursed. Some carriers encourage their owner-operators to paint and letter their trucks in a company color scheme, and pay them extra if they will. But they cannot require them to because it would violate the owner-operators' status as independent contractors—a legal status that affects how and what taxes are paid.

You have to determine if those loads or contracts provide enough revenue to make your business a success.

It is important to remember that although you are an independent businessperson as an owner-operator, you are of value to the company contracting you and your equipment only if you are dependable and reputable. The company that secures the freight for you will be able to solicit that freight only as long as they provide the dependable service the shipper demands. The need for a safe driving record is as important for the owner-operator as for the company driver. Because insurance rates are determined by past performance, and the company you contract with is responsible for you and the freight you haul while under contract, the carrier will not be interested in an owner-operator with a history of accidents or traffic violations.

It would be difficult to give average annual earnings for an owner-operator. As in any other business, there are those who actually lose money, while others do very well. The state of the economy, your business ability, and how hard you are willing to work will determine how much compensation you will receive. For some it will be less than company drivers, for others it could be more.

LOCAL TRUCK DRIVER

Local truck drivers, also known as pickup and delivery drivers, are those who generally get to sleep in their own beds each night. In most instances, they report to work at a local terminal and spend their day delivering and picking up packages and freight for businesses and industries along a specified route within generally short distances from the local terminal. Local drivers also work for merchants and manufacturers, delivering all kinds of goods to homes, stores, and businesses. Food, beverages, fuel, furniture, and office supplies are among the goods handled by such drivers.

While the same driving skills required of an over-the-road driver are necessary for a local driver, the latter spends much more time physically handling freight and less time driving. The local driver may drive only fifty miles a day, compared to the 500-mile day put in by the over-the-road driver.

The local drivers also play a very important role in the company's sales effort. In fact, many companies call them "driver salespeople." The local drivers are the only trucking company employees who have an opportunity for daily contact with the customer. For this reason, the job requires a likeable, outgoing person.

The carriers selected to move freight for a company are generally chosen on the basis of cost and service by traffic executives who are generally a part of the firm's management team. But the people in the shipping department can funnel a lot of freight to a carrier if that carrier has a driver they like. In such a competitive

Local deliveries often use short, twenty-seven- or twenty-eight-foot vans pulled by medium-duty tractors. The short trailers can also be used over-the-road and are commonly seen being pulled two or three at a time by a heavy duty tractor.

industry, the extra freight generated by a motivated driver can be the difference between operating at a profit or a loss.

The importance of the driver salesperson can best be illustrated with the example of a couple of drivers.

One of those drivers, Joe, was from a terminal in a small northern Wisconsin community. Because of an economic slowdown, Joe, who had the least seniority, was laid off. Instead of feeling sorry for himself, he changed his driving uniform for a suit and started knocking on the doors of the shipping docks where he had previously made pickups and deliveries. He told his

25

friends that his company needed to haul more of their freight so that he could get back to work. In less than two weeks he had his job back.

A North Carolina local driver, Harry made a point of making good friends in the shipping departments where he made his pickups. An avid fisherman, Harry regularly arranged fishing trips with his customers. As a result, he generally picked up much more freight at the customer's dock. True, these drivers are not average, but they can serve as examples of how to be a good local driver and a valued employee.

Combination Driver/Loader

Depending on the size of the terminal, local drivers may also have to serve as loaders, which means that when they are not picking up or delivering freight, they are loading and unloading trucks at their terminals. At large terminals, however, the drivers generally come to work in the morning, find their trucks loaded, and take to the street to deliver the freight. When the freight is delivered, the driver may pick up other freight and take it back to the terminal, where a full-time loader unloads the truck. In the case of the large terminal, the loader is probably not a driver at all, but spends the entire day loading and unloading freight.

Persons prone to injury or with back problems should avoid careers as local drivers or loaders. These positions require a substantial amount of manual labor.

Anyone who feels he or she has the qualifications to fill a local driver position or a loader position should visit the various truck terminals in the area and ask the terminal managers for applications. He or she should also visit food processors, distributors and manufacturers operating their own trucks. These companies often provide jobs to people under twenty-one years of age. They also employ driver salespeople who deal with customers in a manner similar to what freight-hauling delivery drivers do.

While the positions are sometimes listed in a local newspaper, the chances of being hired are better if you search out the job. In many cases, the terminal manager may have a file full of applications and never find it necessary to advertise. If you have taken the trouble to have your application in that file and have created the proper impression during your interview, the job could be yours.

Another source for locating such positions is the Teamsters union hall in your city. Generally, when a trucking company has too much work for its regular force, it calls the union for "casual" workers. If the work load remains heavy, those casual positions can become full-time jobs. But remember that unions have diminished in importance since the industry was deregulated.

Like the over-the-road driver, the local driver or combination driver/loader can earn from $8 to $15 per hour.

3

Terminal Operations

There are several types of trucking companies. The type of operation often dictates the type of equipment, the facilities, and the people needed.

Much of this nation's freight is moved by the truckload. Companies called truckload carriers generally have a home office and over-the-road drivers who pick up a complete truckload at a factory or warehouse and deliver that entire load to another store, warehouse, or place of business.

Many businesses, however, cannot use an entire truckload of a given product and therefore order quantities that might weigh from 500 to 10,000 pounds. These smaller shipments are called LTL, or less than truckload shipments. Because the movement of LTL freight plays such an important role in the national economy, many LTL carriers are in operation.

For maximum efficiency, the LTL carriers must consolidate the shipments of several shippers onto one truck headed for a given city. For that reason, they operate out of strategically located facilities called terminals.

A terminal is a building with a concrete dock four feet four inches high, to which trucks can back up for the loading and unloading of freight. The length of the dock varies depending on the needs of the company. In more

The architectural concept shown above is typical of a modern truck freight terminal, with the office and freight dock connected in a T-shaped facility. The typical terminal maintenance facility is also shown behind the dock area.

rural areas, a small terminal with eight- to ten-door docks might be adequate; the same carrier might have 200- to 300-door terminals in larger cities.

Most companies use a cross-dock operation, with doors on both sides of the dock. The over-the-road trucks are placed on one side of the dock and the pickup and delivery units on the other. This type of operation allows for maximum efficiency in the movement of inbound freight from an over-the-road truck to the delivery units, and by the same token the movement of outbound freight from the local pickup unit to the over-the-road trailer.

A terminal usually has an office area and a maintenance facility for repairs and safety checks. The office area would house a terminal manager's office, one or more sales offices, a drivers room, a reception and customer service area, and a dispatcher and supervisor area with a wide window overlooking the dock. The

A freight dock is vital to the operation of a less than truck-load freight operation. The dock is used for sorting and building truckloads for a given destination.

terminal is the home base for several trucking careers. Most of these positions are unique to LTL carriers, since truckload carriers have a home office instead of terminals. The exceptions are customer service representatives and dispatchers, who operate from the home office in the case of truckload carriers.

BILLING CLERK

The most basic entry-level position at the terminal is that of billing clerk. The billing clerk generally works in the late afternoon and early evening hours transmitting information from the terminal to the home office via a computer linkup. This information concerning the freight picked up by that terminal during the day enables rating department employees in the home office to rate the freight and prepare bills. (The rating process is explained in detail in chapters 7 and 8, covering data processing and traffic department positions.)

In small terminals, a high school student is often hired on a part-time basis to handle the billing clerk duties. The student must be sharp, have a concern for detail, and be able to type. An understanding of basic computer language and familiarity with data entry functions can also be important, as computers are used to transmit information from the terminal to the home office.

The fact that the billing clerk position is sometimes filled by a high school student does not minimize the importance of accuracy and excellence in the performance of this vital function. Although it is an entry-level position, a good share of vice presidents and department heads have started in the industry as billing clerks, in many instances as part-timers while they attended high school or college.

The salary for billing clerk may be near the minimum wage during a short training period, but ranges between $6 and $12 per hour once the person understands the job and can work with limited supervision.

A student or young person desiring such a position should submit a résumé to the local terminal manager. Especially in the case of a high school student, the maturity level displayed during the interview is an important determining factor in the hiring decision. Most high schools today offer business courses or career counseling services to help students learn to present themselves in a professional manner. Chapter 14 in this book, "Finding That First Job," may also provide some help in finding and securing this kind of position.

Using a computer link, a customer service representative can provide a customer with almost instant information about a particular shipment.

CUSTOMER SERVICE REPRESENTATIVE

Almost every terminal, regardless of size, employs at least one person who has the title of customer service representative. At a very small terminal, this person may also have other duties. However, the customer service representative job is a key and vital position to any successful trucking company.

The customer service representative must like people and like working with them. He or she must be pleasant and polite, as he or she is constantly working with customers who want information about their shipments. Sometimes a customer with an overdue shipment can be very unpleasant, so a good customer service representative must be composed and professional under pressure.

The workday of a customer service representative includes a substantial amount of time tracing customer shipments, mostly by computer. Many customers today operate production lines from rolling truck inventories (this means parts go directly from the truck to the production line), which must arrive on time or production lines go down. It is therefore understandable that customers want to keep close tabs on their freight.

The customer service representative also works with the customer in cases of shortages or damaged freight. The degree of diplomacy exercised in handling these cases can determine whether or not the company will be able to retain that customer.

Laura

Laura has been a customer service representative at a trucking terminal for the past ten years. She became interested in the industry because her father was a truck driver. She says that her job is very meaningful to her because she has an opportunity to work with customers and help them solve their problems. She says she feels especially good when she can help a customer with a particular service that exceeds the normal expectations.

Laura knows she has an opportunity to help her company by providing customers with information and assurances that the freight shipped via her company will arrive on time and in good condition. That kind of service results in repeat business with those customers. After ten years of that friendly, dependable service, many customers use her company just because they have a great deal of faith in her. Laura says that gives her a special feeling of satisfaction and pride in her job that she probably would not find in many other kinds of work. She says she looks forward to going to work each day and never finds her job boring.

A customer service representative is sometimes considered an entry-level position in the operations field, but it is also an important position that can play a key role in the success or failure of a company. The terminal managers hiring customer service representatives will be especially interested in the personalities of the applicants and how they handle themselves during the interviews. A young person seeking a position as a customer service representative should have a high school diploma and typing and basic computer skills.

An experienced customer service representative can expect to earn between $7 and $12 per hour. The size of the city where the terminal is located and the volume of business determines the rate of pay.

DISPATCHER

The title of dispatcher can actually cover two different jobs. The first is that of the local terminal dispatcher, who makes sure the local freight is delivered in the most efficient manner possible. He or she is also responsible for picking up the freight that local businesses and industries want to ship and getting it back to the terminal.

A local dispatcher works with two groups of people: his or her local drivers and the customers who call in the shipments.

Dispatchers must be well organized and able to handle pressure. To be most effective, they must be respected and liked by their drivers. A good dispatcher can save the company a substantial amount of money by coordinating deliveries and pickups with as little driving as possible. In larger cities, dispatchers must have a good working knowledge of how to get around so they can move their drivers in the fastest possible manner.

The ability of dispatchers to be a positive company contact for customers is also extremely important. Many customers probably talk on the phone with them daily. For customers to continue to call the company, they must feel good about that daily conversation and trust the dispatcher's professional ability. A customer may call with a shipment for St. Louis, Minnesota. A knowledgeable dispatcher will know if that customer also has freight headed for Dallas, Texas, Chicago, Illinois or any other city, and will ask if the driver can also pick up that shipment. Often they will be successful, and their company will have gained extra business.

A person seeking a career as a local dispatcher should have a high school education and some of the distinguishing qualities mentioned earlier in this chapter. To arrange for an interview for such a position, you would make an appointment with the terminal manager. The average annual salary for local dispatchers ranges from $30,000 to $35,000.

The second dispatch position is the over-the-road dispatcher, who is generally located in a central home office rather than at a terminal location. The main function of an over-the-road dispatcher is to coordinate drivers and equipment needed to move freight between cities. That sounds like a relatively easy job, but it requires much coordination and can cause substantial frustration.

At times, over-the-road dispatchers have more loads of freight to move than they have drivers available to move them. In such cases, they must decide which loads are the most important and move them first. The problem becomes even greater if several of those trailers are loaded with freight that is scheduled for delivery at a designated time to keep production lines operating in factories. Computers and sophisticated software, along with mobile communications, have allowed smaller numbers of dispatchers to supervise larger groups of drivers. Where one dispatcher may have been assigned twenty-five drivers previously, now he or she may supervise 100. And instructions may be relayed to drivers by computerized messages instead of by phone conversations. It all works much faster and cuts administrative costs, even if it "depersonalizes" communications somewhat.

Dispatchers may also face a situation in which there are ten loads moving into St. Louis but only two coming out, and two loads going to Nashville, Tennessee but eight to move out. They are charged with getting the job done in the most efficient way, realizing that every time they move one of their drivers in an empty truck, those are nonrevenue-producing miles that impair their company's profitability.

Like local dispatchers, the over-the-road dispatchers must have positive relationships with their drivers. They may be the only people from the company that drivers talk to for an entire week. How drivers feel about their company on a given day, their concern for safety and safe driving habits, and their general outlook on life may all be tied to the mood set by the dispatcher in their latest contact with each other.

As you can see, a good trucking company is really a team effort, with each employee playing a key role and all of the positions being interdependent.

A person seeking an over-the-road dispatching position should arrange an interview with the company's director of central dispatch. A high school education and the other character traits mentioned earlier are vital to this position. Some training positions are available in the over-the-road dispatch field, but many companies require some industry background and experience.

Like the local dispatcher, the average annual salary is $30,000 to $35,000.

DOCK FOREPERSON/SUPERVISOR

The team effort involved in the expeditious and profitable movement of freight includes dock forepersons or supervisors.

The dock forepersons are responsible for the proper loading and unloading of freight at the terminals. They supervise and schedule the dockworkers. Over-the-road trucks arriving at the terminal often contain freight for a number of customers, who may be located on several different pickup and delivery routes. Thus, the contents of one large trailer may need to be placed in three or four local trailers for the final trip to the customer. In the scheduling of this work, the dock supervisor must work closely with the dispatcher so that the local driver's truck is loaded and ready to go when the driver reports to work.

The same is true of freight picked up by local drivers that must be reloaded into the over-the-road trailer. The supervisor oversees the process to make sure the trailer is properly loaded. Improper loading could result in the load shifting in transit and freight being damaged. The supervisor is also responsible for making sure the trailer contains as much freight as it can legally carry. If it is not loaded to near capacity, the company's profitability suffers. If more freight is loaded into the trailer than it can legally haul, the company can be fined if the truck is checked at a law-enforcement scale.

Placement of the freight in the trailer is also vital to the operation, and a great deal of planning is required. The trailer may carry one or several shipments that are to be dropped en route. An example might be a trailer moving from Atlanta, Georgia to Minneapolis, Minnesota. If the freight to be dropped off first is

37

Dock supervisors check each load to assure the trailer contains the right amount of weight for the maximum profit for his company.

improperly loaded in the back of the trailer, and it cannot be reached without unloading the whole truck, the shipment may have to go all the way to Minneapolis and then be shipped back. Obviously, such a mistake would be costly for the trucking company, which has to handle that freight a second time for free. It could also result in a very unhappy customer if that particular shipment was needed to keep his or her production line operating.

The dock supervisor must also be well trained in safe freight-handling practices to eliminate costly accidents and injuries on the dock.

A high school diploma would satisfy the educational requirements for a dock supervisor position. A person seeking such a position would generally need experience as a dockworker. The ability to work with and supervise people, to plan ahead, and to assure the proper loading of trailers are qualities necessary for success as a dock supervisor. The average salary of dock supervisors ranges from $25,000 to $30,000 a year.

OPERATIONS MANAGER

If a terminal is not operated in a smooth and profitable manner, it is of little benefit to the trucking company. The operations manager is charged with making sure the operation is both smooth and profitable.

A good operations manager makes sure that the company's customers receive excellent service. However, the manager must also make sure that the service being provided is generating a profit for his or her company. With the assistance of computer printouts and productivity formulas, the managers can determine if they have enough people to handle the work load.

If they keep the workforce too lean, profits might be temporarily enhanced but service will deteriorate and customers will be lost. If the number of employees is too great in relation to the number of shipments, their operation costs the company money. Since a roller-coaster pattern of freight availability is common in the industry, good operations managers must be flexible, and have the courage to trim their work force during business dips and the ability to plan for the peaks.

39

An operations manager must like working with people, but must be assertive enough to manage them. He or she must also be comfortable working with reports and computer-generated data.

A high school diploma may meet the educational requirements for a career as an operations manager, but a college degree in business administration with appropriate transportation courses could enhance promotion to more lucrative industry positions. The salary for an operations manager varies with the size of the operation, from $30,000 to $40,000.

TERMINAL MANAGER

If the various industry positions discussed thus far are all key team positions, the terminal manager would be the coach. The manager is the one who has to bring it all together, deals with day-to-day problems that may come up, and is charged with making sure the terminal is profitable.

The terminal manager generally reports to a regional manager and follows certain operating procedures sent down from the home office. But despite that, the managers are running their own profit center. The payroll of the terminal can range from five to 500 employees. A terminal manager must know the industry and usually has held one or more of the positions already covered in this book. Because sales and the understanding of sales are so vital, most terminal managers have spent some time as an industry sales representative. However, other terminal managers come through the operations side and advance from driver, dispatcher, or customer service representative.

Although not a prerequisite in the past, some companies may now require their terminal managers to have a college degree with emphasis on business administration and transportation. The position demands a personality that can win the respect of employees as well as customers.

To be successful, terminal managers have to get maximum productivity from their drivers and dockworkers and generate that same productivity in their sales and office staff. The secret seems to be in setting high but realistic expectations and getting everyone excited about being part of a winning team.

To emphasize the importance of this position, consider two terminals that had dramatic changes in their profitability. One of those terminals was located in a small Indiana community with a substantial amount of industry in the surrounding area. The company that opened the terminal watched it lose money as two successive managers tried to run it. The third manager was promoted from a sales position and seemed to have the right stuff. He was well liked by the customers, worked hard, and created an infectious winning attitude among his employees. In a very short time, that small terminal was boasting the best profit on percentage of revenue as well as the third-largest gross revenue for the entire company. The drivers had the highest regard for their terminal manager and were convinced he would take them to number one in the company. He was promoted to regional manager of another region before that goal was achieved.

The second example was a big-city terminal that had been losing money for many years. The employees had extremely low self-esteem until the right manager was hired. Again, in a very short time the terminal started showing a profit. The terminal manager was able to turn the operation around by setting goals for the employees and getting them to believe in themselves. The employees couldn't help but be successful when they started to follow the professional, winning pace set by their manager.

While there are those who assume that a good terminal manager is one who is good at giving orders, the most successful terminal managers, in fact, lead by example. They work hard and smart, and they expect and get the same from their employees.

If you possess some of the qualities of the managers in those two success stories, the trucking industry needs you. You will be amply rewarded for your contributions to the industry. The annual salary for terminal managers can vary from $30,000 to $100,000. The size of the terminal is also a factor.

REGIONAL MANAGER

The management link between the home office and the various terminals in the field is the regional or district manager. The title depends on the company in question. Some companies have district sales managers and regional operations managers. Because the two functions, sales and operations, are closely related, many companies have a regional manager who is experienced in both.

The exact functions of regional managers can vary, but generally they are in regular contact with the vice president of sales and operations in the home office. Their purpose is to make sure that the various programs and types of operations the home office desires are implemented in the field. The terminals under their jurisdiction are generally located in a given area; however, the position still requires substantial travel.

The regional manager is usually involved in the hiring, training, and promotion of key terminal-level people. They are also responsible for monitoring, on a daily basis, the progress of the terminals in their region. With the assistance of computer reports, they can tell whether sales goals are being met and budgets are being kept.

In many instances, the regional manager joins the terminal salespeople on sales calls.

A person who advances to the position of regional manager generally has a very outgoing personality, must motivate the people in management positions at the terminal level, and has an overall positive influence that reaches all the way to the drivers who stop at the customer's door. Trucking is very much a people business, and the positive people in the business are the most successful.

Salaries for regional managers vary depending on the number of terminals in the district and the company in question. Their salaries are larger than those of the terminal managers and sales executives under their jurisdiction.

MODERN TECHNOLOGY

Sophisticated computers and satellite communications will be among the tools used in most of the operations positions listed.

The competitive nature of the industry dictates that a good manager must have the assistance of computers for accurately assessing freight costs, resource management, and equipment utilization and scheduling.

Dispatchers communicate with drivers thousands of miles away via satellite, such as a mobile phone. That permits the most expeditious movement of power and equipment. It also makes it possible for the dispatcher to know exactly where a given truck is and when it will arrive at the loading dock.

Operations people keep track of loads and where they are by computer. Much paperwork is now scanned into the computer systems of trucking companies and shippers and receivers so operators can see the actual paperwork. Some freight drivers send bills of lading and other paperwork to their home offices with a mobile facsimile machine right in their truck cabs. This means the billing process can start immediately, rather than waiting until the end of the day, or perhaps days later. This speeds up the flow of revenues, making the company more efficient.

Drivers working for package delivery companies carry hand-held computers that resemble clipboards; they use these to report the delivery of individual shipments and even get the signatures of people receiving the shipments as proof that shipments were delivered. Mainframe computer systems store data so packages and express letters can be tracked continuously. So important are the computers, that stand-by power systems take over if commercial electricity fails. Obviously, the computers themselves require highly trained technicians to program and maintain them. If you're interested in computers, you may someday find yourself working in the trucking industry.

4

Sales and Marketing

Perhaps one of the most challenging jobs in trucking today is freight sales. A sales career in trucking differs in a number of ways from the careers of most people selling goods and services.

To start with, it is one of the few sales careers that offers a fixed salary rather than a commission. Although several trucking firms offer bonuses or sales incentives, for the most part, the industry's salespeople work on a fixed salary.

Trucking companies have good reasons not to put strong emphasis on commissions. First, it is difficult to measure the true production of an industry sales executive. If you sell cars or vacuum cleaners it is quite simple to determine a commission on the amount of revenue you generate in a day or a week. Not so in freight sales.

Let us assume you are a trucking sales executive in Los Angeles, and you have a shipper that does $10,000 worth of business with your terminal each week. Then one day the account starts doing $25,000 of business weekly. It may be proper to credit you for the increased business, or the credit may belong to one of your company's St. Paul, Minnesota sales representatives who persuaded the receiver of the freight to specify your company on all shipments. By the same token, that $10,000 weekly business may drop to nothing because a St. Paul operations person let a shipment sit on a dock for several days and forced the receiver of the goods to shut down a factory. Many other intangibles have an impact on the customer you call on. For instance, the customer may like or dislike the driver you have picking up his or her freight.

Regardless of why a shipper uses a certain trucking company, the trucking sales representative is a vital part of the operation. A successful company has a force of bright, energetic sales executives who know their customers' needs and their company's ability to meet those needs.

The salesperson's abilities are key to the success of any company. The lack of a commission need not be a concern for a person who is confident that he or she is a top performer. If you are really that good, your salary will reflect that performance. In this industry the word spreads quickly, and a top salesperson receives offers from every other carrier in town. If your employer wants to keep you, the salary has to give you a reason to stay.

How to Succeed

A person who chooses a career in freight sales must have a likable personality. It is not unusual for several trucking companies to offer the same service at the same price, so in the end the purchaser could well base his or her decision on likes and dislikes. However, a good personality is not enough. You also have to be knowledgeable and able to understand as well as explain complex tariffs and how the customer can benefit from using your company. You have to be tactful enough to persuade the customer to use your company for the needs that your company can serve, while also helping the customer find other outlets for those needs you cannot readily serve. That way you will not lose the entire account. Your career involves more than just selling; it's also helping the customer solve his or her distribution problems.

Entertainment plays an important role in freight sales. While the ability to play golf, tennis, and other one-on-one sports is not a must, it can certainly be a plus. If you like to put in a day of work and go home and have the evening to yourself, a career in freight sales is probably not for you. Successful salespeople in this industry try to get close to their customers. Entertainment is one of the best methods to achieve that goal. That often means dinners, ball games, and social events that may include spouses.

Often a good trucking company sales executive develops lasting friendships with the traffic managers who make the decisions on what trucking company to use. You will have the opportunity to meet and get to know some wonderful people in this career. You will also have to entertain and be nice to some unappreciative shipping executives who know you need their business and may abuse your hospitality. Like any other career, trucking has a few negatives to go along with a lot more positives.

A successful freight sales executive is also a careful person who keeps accurate records, follows computerized data to see how much business a customer is doing with the company, and keeps tabs on the movement of that customer's freight to make sure it is delivered in the most expeditious way possible.

A person in a freight sales career must enjoy working with people and helping people. The way a sales executive dresses is very important too, as the customer often judges the company by the appearance of the salesperson. A rep dressed in fresh, clean, sharp clothes creates a feeling of success, and most shippers prefer to ship their goods via a successful carrier.

Because sales play such a key role in the competitive trucking industry, successful sales executives can generally count on promotion to positions as terminal manager and area or regional manager. There is also room on the top few rungs of the executive ladder for those who really shine. A great deal of work and dedication is required of those hoping to reach the top of the ladder.

Sales Opportunities for Women

Sales and marketing is probably the fastest growing area for women seeking careers in what used to be an almost all-male industry. With more and more businesses and manufacturing firms hiring and promoting women in their shipping and traffic departments, it is only natural that the trucking industry is also turning to women for its sales executive positions.

Judy

Judy is a woman in freight sales who decided to enter the industry at age thirty-nine. She had been serving as a distribution manager for a Southern manufacturing firm and felt that she needed a new challenge.

Her decision to seek a career as a sales executive in the trucking industry was the result of encouragement she received from a friend in the industry, who told her she had the personality to be successful in sales. Judy says that her lack of sales experience made finding that first job a little more difficult, but that she was determined and her perseverance resulted in success.

Judy notes that there are substantially more men than women freight sales executives, and that there are also more male customers. She has found that acceptance in the industry is not based on gender, but on professional ability and performance. She says she has never regretted her decision to seek the new challenges of this

An industrial traffic manager (above left) discusses her shipping needs with a trucking company sales executive during a sales call.

industry. For her it has been a most rewarding career. She says she has found some of the nicest people in the world in the corporate traffic departments she visits daily.

Her recommendation to other women or men who might consider a career as a trucking industry freight sales executive: "If you like meeting people and have the personality to ask for their business, a most rewarding lifestyle is yours."

While many companies seek experienced sales executives with established customer bases, only a limited number of experienced people are available, so openings exist for energetic new people who desire to succeed. Also, some companies prefer inexperienced

49

sales representatives whom they can train in ways that have proven successful for them.

Is Sales for You?

A candidate for a sales position would be in a most advantageous position with a résumé that included a college degree or an associate degree in marketing, with some traffic and transportation courses. Any sales experience, even if not related to freight sales, would be beneficial.

Your résumé should be filed with the various terminal managers who have operations in the community where you would like to work. In some instances, hiring of sales representatives is done by the vice president of sales, who may be in the home office far from the terminal. Therefore, it might be to your advantage to send a résumé to the vice president of sales if you desire employment with a particular company. Any contact or relationship you have with customers of the prospective employer should be noted on your résumé or application.

Starting salaries in freight sales range from $25,000 to $30,000, perhaps more in cities with high costs of living. It is not unusual for experienced sales executives to have annual salaries of $30,000 to $40,000, and well in excess of that for sales executives who have a proven track record.

Inside Sales

Many trucking companies have expanded their coverage to forty-eight states. Often it is not economically feasible to set up terminals and sales offices in all of those locations. When their trucks haul freight to a destination where there is no company facility, it is still necessary to find a return load. This has given rise to a truck marketing activity called inside sales.

Often inside sales employees follow a prepared presentation. The ability to be pleasant and convincing on the telephone is the most important qualification. Obviously, appearance and other factors vital in the one-on-one type of sales have little importance in inside sales. Also, your salary in inside sales would not be as high as that of the one-on-one sales executive who makes personal calls. The pay ranges from $6 to $12 an hour.

Companies looking for inside sales employees generally advertise in local newspapers. Not all trucking companies utilize inside sales, so only a limited number of these positions are presently available.

Preparing for a Sales Career

Persons considering a career in freight sales should take advantage of as many sales seminars and training sessions as possible.

The sophisticated operations and needs of those who will be purchasing your service are increasing every day. To be successful, you too must offer sophisticated shipping ideas and strategies.

Product knowledge, good service, and dependability are vitally important in freight sales; also, the way you package what you have to sell will play an important role in your success.

Training to help you become a better presenter can often be helpful before you join the industry.

5

Maintaining Equipment

Trucks must be maintained carefully so they run efficiently and reliably. Depending on how it's outfitted, a highway tractor can cost $65,000 to $100,000 or more, and a simple van-type trailer can be priced at $15,000. More specialized equipment, like a trash truck with its hydraulically operated packer body, or an insulated tank trailer that carries super-cold gasses, can cost $150,000 to $300,000. These costly investments must be protected.

Equipment maintenance is very important and requires highly trained and motivated people. Some of the positions described in the following pages are available in trucking and other companies. The truck technician, for example, can also be found in outside maintenance organizations, including independent shops, dealers, and leasing companies.

One thing to note is that in recent years, manufacturers of truck components have made many improvements to make the equipment last far longer than it used to. For example, where a heavy-duty diesel truck once ran only a half-million miles before needing an overhaul, vehicle life of 900,000 to more than 1 million miles is now common. Transmissions and axles that use to run a million miles before major work was needed now last even longer. So less heavy maintenance is needed than before.

Also, many over-the-road fleets now trade their equipment often to keep it "young." Like automobiles, newer trucks are more reliable than old ones, and get better fuel economy. New trucks are also more pleasant to drive. This attracts good drivers and helps a company overcome the chronic driver shortage. Motor carriers commonly trade truck-tractors every three to five years, and, in that time, only minor maintenance is needed. Carriers with these fleets have only small maintenance shops.

Who buys this traded-in equipment? Smaller fleets and owner-operators. Eventually more major repairs and overhauls are needed, so shops and mechanics— who are now usually called "technicians" because they deal with high-tech equipment—are still needed. Maintenance work is highly demanding and requires special skills. But it generally pays more than driving because there has always been a shortage of good technicians.

In trucking companies, a number of key maintenance positions exist. Bear in mind, however, that much of today's maintenance is done in outside shops where the level of service is often higher than in the fleets themselves.

Truck Technician

Since the great majority of all equipment utilized by the industry is diesel-powered, a person working to maintain that equipment needs to be trained in diesel mechanics. Also, most diesels now have electronic controls, which require entirely new skills of technicians. The technician must be able to work with a small computer to diagnose engine troubles. Among other things, he or she must be able to read well and comprehend the readings because following instructions found in the computer programs and manuals is an important part of the job. Those who attend a technical school learn what's needed to work on modern diesels and trucks. A degree from a technical school is almost always necessary in getting an industry position.

Some companies have shops at all of their major terminal locations, so jobs can generally be found without relocating. A job at a terminal shop usually involves routine maintenance to keep the trucks safe and in good running condition. Safety is very important in the industry. It is regular practice by successful carriers for every unit to go through a safety check lane before heading out for a trip. During this safety test, tires, hoses, belts, brakes, lights, and other safety features are checked. No cost-conscious carrier can afford to have a $100,000 unit involved in an accident because the brakes were not properly checked. Most carriers have also found that it is less costly to make sure the equipment leaves in excellent condition than to try to fix breakdowns when they occur on the highway. In addition to the expense of moving your mechanics to the scene of the breakdown or paying an outside service firm for that repair work, you have the pay of the waiting driver who goes on the clock at up to $16 per hour while his or her equipment is repaired on the road.

A terminal-level maintenance employee must be able to work with people, such as the drivers who use the equipment. It is usually the drivers who let the maintenance worker know when a unit is defective.

The terminal-level maintenance employee should expect some night work, since over-the-road trucks are usually driven during the night. If a breakdown occurs near your terminal, you might also be called out at night to get the unit back on the road.

Most of the larger carriers have a centralized maintenance facility for major repairs. The diesel mechanics who work at these facilities may be involved in rebuilding entire engines, transmissions, fuel systems, or various electronic parts. In addition to a technical degree, these rebuild specialists often have to take special maintenance seminars, usually sponsored by the manufacturing firm that supplies the company with its equipment. The modern, energy-efficient equipment has so much electronic and computer equipment that it can be properly maintained only by a person who keeps up to date on the technology involved in the construction of a particular part.

Diesel mechanics working for a modern trucking company are seldom bored, as the new equipment constantly provides new challenges.

Jack's Job

Jack has been a diesel mechanic for seventeen years. He entered the industry after spending several years as an auto mechanic. He says that he always held a special interest in the big trucks, and he has never regretted making the decision to get into truck maintenance. Each day and each truck present a new challenge. Jack says he never has any trouble getting out of bed and going to work because he truly loves what he does.

Jack sees the role of the mechanic as basic to the operation of a trucking company. As he puts it, "You can't go very far if the equipment isn't kept in top shape."

Asked if there are any negatives to the diesel mechanic position, Jack says there is one. At one point early in his career he left the industry for a few months because he didn't like constantly being dirty and having greasy hands. While that is something Jack feels somewhat uncomfortable with, his love for his job and his belief that he is doing something important makes it

55

The skills needed to rebuild diesel engines, as well as other mechanical components, provide a challenge for those seeking careers as diesel mechanics.

possible for him to overlook the discomfort. He says there is no chance that he will ever consider getting out of the business again.

According to Jack, young people who feel they might like careers as diesel mechanics should get a good technical education in that field. He acknowledges that most major carriers prefer to hire experienced mechanics, but says that a determined young person can always find a job with a small shop or small trucking company.

Once experience has been acquired, the diesel mechanic generally has quite a bit of job security, because someone always seems to need a good diesel mechanic. A simple curriculum for a sound training course is listed in Appendix I.

Salaries for diesel mechanics vary with the type of company. A range of $10 to $20 per hour can be expected. A person seeking such a job should present a résumé, with appropriate documentation of work experience, to the shop superintendent or the director of maintenance.

PARTS MANAGER

Another key position in the maintenance department is the parts manager. This person makes sure that parts are always on hand and ready for the mechanic who needs them to get a piece of equipment back into revenue-producing condition and on the road.

Because the average-size carrier uses equipment from several suppliers, virtually thousands of different parts must be available in the company's central parts inventory. To keep track of all those parts, many companies have adopted a computerized inventory system. This helps the parts manager know what is available at the various terminal shops and quickly retrieve a needed part. Failure to have parts ready when needed is generally costly for the company, as the mechanic who needs the parts may be in the middle of a job and be forced to drop it until the parts arrive.

The parts manager spends a good deal of time meeting with vendors who want to supply the parts the company needs. For this reason, the parts manager must have the mechanic's technical knowledge plus some business, purchasing, and computer knowledge.

BODY MECHANIC

With the high purchase cost of tractors or trailers, they are seldom discarded if they become involved in accidents. Most medium- to large-sized carriers have their own body shop and employ body repair experts who can virtually rebuild a tractor or trailer from the frame up. Technical training for truck body repair is available; however, the training alone does not assure one of the skills needed to be successful. The really good body repairer is aware of equipment appearance: the tractors and trailers put back in service have to be in like-new condition.

The same salary schedule used for the company's diesel mechanics usually applies to the body repair experts.

TIRE REPAIR SPECIALIST

Since most large trucks have eighteen wheels, thousands of tires are needed annually to keep an average carrier rolling.

Carriers usually do not discard tires when the original tread is worn. New treads are added into old, worn tires in a process called recapping. In company recapping facilities, tires are recapped one to three times. Recapping, even with the labor involved, is substantially cheaper than purchasing new tires. Each recapping gives tires over 100,000 miles of life.

The recapping process is quite repetitive, and persons seeking such a job should be aware of that. In most cases, the tire department employees belong to the same union as the mechanics, so a comparable salary can be expected.

SHOP SUPERINTENDENT

The coordination, scheduling, and inspection of work performed by the mechanics is the function of the shop superintendent.

Obviously, to be successful a superintendent must have substantial experience as a mechanic.

The position requires some decision-making as to which repairs are the most vital to the company's operation and the appropriate prioritizing of those jobs. The shop superintendent may also have to help a mechanic who is having trouble solving a particular maintenance problem.

The salary exceeds that of the mechanic, but varies depending on the size of the shop and the number of employees under supervision. Leadership qualities and the ability to work with people are musts for this position.

SERVICE WRITER

Truck and engine dealers have service writers who act in much the same way as their counterparts at automobile dealers. A service writer greets truck drivers or other fleet employees as they come in, then listens to and writes out their complaints. The service writer has to interpret the complaints, converting symptoms into likely causes or problems, then assign the truck to the first available technician who's capable of repairing it. This sometimes requires experience as a mechanic or technician, or specialized training to make decisions based on the information available. Sometimes clues are available in a computer record that keeps track of the truck's maintenance history.

Even more important are the service writer's "people" skills. This is a customer service job. He or she has to deal with people who are sometimes angry at the trouble the "broken" truck is causing, as well as deal with the pressure to get it fixed fast and back on the road. Many of today's drivers are not paid while they wait for repairs, so they can be very impatient. You have to enjoy working with people, be able to understand and sympathize with their predicaments, and get satisfaction from making them feel better by helping to solve their equipment problems.

DIRECTOR OF MAINTENANCE

The director of maintenance is almost always a member of the management team and often is a vice president.

This person writes the specifications for new equipment, negotiates with suppliers, and makes the ultimate purchase decisions. The director of maintenance can save or cost the company millions of dollars with those purchases. Unlike automobiles, which have standard equipment, two trucks can look identical because the cab is made by a certain supplier, but have no similar features beyond that outside shell. The director of maintenance writes the specifications for the truck engine, transmission, axles, and numerous other components based on how the equipment is to be used. A company that hauls a lot of light but bulky freight might use entirely different tractors and trailers than a company that handles heavy dense freight. The specifications could also vary if the trucks have to travel mountainous routes rather than on flat, even highways.

Decisions on the purchase of fuel, oil, and tires are also under the maintenance director's jurisdiction.

In addition to general responsibilities of the entire company's maintenance operation, the director of maintenance attends driver meetings to talk about purchases of new equipment and how to use it properly.

Salaries for directors of maintenance vary substantially. A company with a $100 million equipment inventory would obviously pay more than one with $10 million or $25 million worth of equipment.

Directors of maintenance get to their positions either by rising through the ranks, from mechanic/technician or parts specialist into management, or by going directly into management after being hired. Managers at this level have shown a high degree of skill at dealing with and supervising people and generally need a college degree in today's job market.

Each fleet needs only one director of maintenance, and many fleets—especially those that trade their equipment often and don't have shops—have reduced this function to one of scheduling and working with outside shops. Still, there are a lot of trucking companies out there and someone has to oversee maintenance. Becoming a director of maintenance is a possibility if you have ambition and business knowledge.

Properties Control

Since some LTL trucking companies have many terminals, it is necessary to have an employee who oversees the maintenance and upkeep of those facilities. The position has various titles depending on the company. Director of terminals, facilities and maintenance director, or some similar title covers this position.

The primary duties include coordination and approval of required repairs or remodeling of facilities in the system. In some companies, the job may also include purchasing new facilities when the company expands or overseeing the construction of new facilities.

The background of the person who fills the position can vary almost as much as the title. The position may be filled by a former terminal manager who has excelled in the maintenance of facilities, or by a former contractor who was involved in the construction of terminals. It could also be an architect or engineer who earns the position.

Whatever the background or title, the position has increasing importance in an age when energy conservation, safety, and efficiency play roles in the success of a business. Many companies have greatly increased their coverage area, so the added facilities give added importance to such a position.

TERMINAL MAINTENANCE TECHNICIAN

Because some maintenance problems are unique to the type of facilities used by the trucking industry, a number of companies now employ mobile facility maintenance crews that travel to and handle the maintenance needs of the various company-owned terminals.

To be a terminal maintenance technician requires basic knowledge and experience in the electrical, welding, concrete, carpentry, plumbing, and heating ventilating air conditioning (HVAC) trades. The technician needs to be well rounded and able to handle overhead door repairs, minor masonry work, installation of light fixtures and receptacles, minor plumbing repairs, maintenance of dockboards, preventive maintenance on heating and cooling equipment, minor roof repairs, and interior and exterior painting.

Travel is a must for this position. Depending on the company you work for, you may have to spend several consecutive weeks on the road. Obviously, you would have to like or tolerate motel living. You would also have to like people, as you would be working with—and, in a sense, for—all of the terminal managers in the system. While your orders would come from the director of facilities and maintenance in the home office, who has to approve all repairs, you would need to work with the terminal manager of the facility.

The salary range is $26,000 to $31,000 per year.

6

Safety, Risk Management, Human Services

The functions of safety, risk management, and human services often come under one department in most trucking companies. That department is usually headed by a vice president.

Safety has always been important to the industry, and in the future that importance can become greater. There are several very good reasons for its increased importance, and insurance is probably on top of the list.

In the mid-1980s, the trucking industry was hit with a crisis that literally put many companies out of business because they could not obtain insurance, or because the cost of insurance was so high that the company could no longer be competitive. Carriers that did not implement sound safety programs were simply denied any insurance, as many insurance underwriters who had suffered large losses, due to liability awards, stopped underwriting trucking companies.

The few insurers that continued to underwrite trucking companies were selective about companies they would cover. Only those with excellent safety records were able to obtain coverage, and even for them the premiums for coverage were substantially increased. Because of this, carriers became aware that any sloppiness in safety programs could result in no coverage or coverage at a cost that would prevent the carrier from being successful in a competitive market.

The image of the industry is a second reason for an increased emphasis on safety. After losing several legislative battles and facing a constant threat of increased taxation, the industry goal has become trying to educate the general public about trucks and their important role in the nation's economy. To accomplish this goal, the industry must deal with truck drivers who speed, drive recklessly, scare motorists by tailgating, or in any other way contradict the "knight of the road" image the industry is attempting to create. It is felt that the best method of dealing with these bad drivers (actually a very small percentage of all of the drivers on the road) are good safety programs.

Safety programs are generally established by the vice president of safety and personnel, but are implemented by a group of employees known as safety managers.

SAFETY MANAGER

The safety manager generally works in a central location with terminals and/or employees under his or her jurisdiction.

The safety manager handles the written and road testing of driver candidates. He or she may also be called to the scene when a company driver is involved in an accident. The safety manager holds safety meetings with the drivers, participates in road patrols to observe the behavior of the company's drivers firsthand, and often meets with the drivers over coffee at truckstops just to talk about safety.

The safety manager generally has audio visual presentations available on such subjects as defensive driving, the proper handling of hazardous materials, avoiding back injuries while handling freight, and others that promote on-the-job safety. He or she also makes certain that safety regulations are followed to the letter so that the company is always in compliance.

The safety manager is almost always a former driver, with a great deal of concern for safety and the ability to communicate and teach his or her fellow truckers. A high school education is a must, and continued education is common.

CHUCK

Chuck was an over-the-road truck driver for seventeen years before he sought a position as a safety manager. He said he was looking for new challenges and felt there were things he could do to improve safety in the industry. "As a driver, you get a view of how things could be done differently, and I felt I could make a contribution as a safety manager." Chuck is concerned with the industry's image and how that image is damaged by just a few drivers who don't adhere to safe driving practices. More than that, however, he is concerned about what might happen to his company's ability to get insurance coverage if the number of accidents gets too high.

Working with people and on accident investigations are interesting aspects of the position for Chuck. While getting out of bed in the middle of the night and going to the scene of an accident isn't Chuck's favorite part of his job, he is satisfied that he made the right choice when he decided to change his career from driver to safety manager. He says he always found great satisfaction driving the big rigs and knowing the freight he was moving was generating revenue for his company. Now, he gets the same feeling from the dollars that can be saved by preventing injuries and accidents. The opportunity to help the people he used to drive with also provides satisfaction for a person who has always had a great deal of pride in the trucking industry.

Chuck predicts that the industry will see a great deal of improvement in safety performance, but that the improvement will also mean a lot of hard work for all those involved in safety.

RISK-MANAGEMENT MANAGER

The manager of risk management generally administers the workers' compensation program, while another person, usually a manager or a supervisor, oversees the employee medical and dental programs, and yet another person, also usually a manager or a supervisor, handles the unemployment compensation program. In the past, these jobs may have been handled by one person, and in some small trucking companies they still are, but in medium- to large-sized companies, these jobs are too complex to be coordinated by a single person.

In many companies, the manager of risk management also negotiates with the providers of liability and casualty insurance concerning cost of premiums and the amount of coverage to be purchased, although federal and state regulations usually provide for a minimum amount of coverage. In larger trucking companies, the company may be self-insured to a certain maximum, in which case the manager of risk management has full authority over settlements.

This is seldom an entry-level job. In addition to a college education, the risk-management manager needs experience either with an insurance company or in a related field where a knowledge of terms and insurance practices can be gained. Salary is dependent on the size of the company and the experience of the person seeking the position. Obviously, in view of the importance of finding insurance coverage and negotiating favorable rates to help a carrier succeed in a competitive industry, companies demand experience and a track record of performance for this important position.

Vice President of Safety and Personnel

The vice president of safety and personnel oversees all safety and insurance matters. He or she formulates and administers programs of selection, training, supervision, record maintenance, and reporting to regulatory agencies. A college degree and a human resources background are requisites for this position.

While all of the responsibilities of this post are important, selection and screening of employees is a function that can have significant impact on the quality and makeup of the company. Safety and personnel is seldom considered a revenue-enhancing department, but this vice president can play a very important role in the profit picture since every dollar paid out for injury or accident comes right out of the profits the company has generated.

Personnel Clerk

The only real entry-level position in the human resources department is that of the personnel clerk.

A high school education with secretarial and office machine skills is required for such a position.

Daily record-keeping and updating of personnel files are two of the most common functions of this position. The ability to work with people is a must. The number of personnel clerks needed depends on the number of employees in the company. Salaries range from $7 to $12 per hour.

Industrial Relations

Trucking companies whose employees are members of the International Brotherhood of Teamsters generally have a department known as industrial relations. In nonunion carriers these functions are often part of the safety and personnel department.

The industrial relations department usually has only a director, an assistant director, and a secretary. The size of the staff, however, does not reflect the importance of the department. Since almost 70¢ of every dollar taken in by a trucking company goes toward employee salaries and benefits, industrial relations is in fact a vital function for a successful carrier.

The union contract, which establishes wages and working conditions for drivers of union companies, is a nationally negotiated contract and is known as the Master Freight Agreement. While the industrial relations director is not a part of the actual negotiating process for that national contract, he or she is involved in bargaining for supplemental agreements that the individual companies negotiate for their own special circumstances. There may also be other unions representing employees. Those contracts are usually negotiated by the director of industrial relations.

Probably the most important duties of the industrial relations director are the understanding and interpretation of the Master Freight Agreement. Although it is negotiated at a national level, the individual companies that sign it must follow it. Not only must the industrial relations director understand the contract, but he or she must make sure that all the terminal managers and other operating officials fully understand it as well. If a union employee believes that the company is not living up to the contract, that employee can file a grievance. In the grievance process, a hearing is held to examine the facts and a grievance committee settles the dispute.

A good industrial relations director seeks to avoid grievances by working closely with the terminal managers and making sure they have a good relationship with their subordinates. Further, he or she makes sure that all warning letters and other disciplinary actions follow the contract to the letter.

Even in the best of situations however, grievances do arise. Since the industrial relations director generally attends grievance hearings with the terminal managers, the position requires a great deal of travel. It obviously also requires a person who is diplomatic and communicates well.

While not always true in the past, industrial relations directors and assistants will probably need a college degree with some law courses. Considerable industry knowledge and experience are necessary to be effective in these positions. A background in the safety or personnel departments, or as a terminal manager who excels in labor relations is needed for this job.

The salary varies with the size of the company, but the position has a top management status, and often the director of industrial relations is a company vice president.

End Result

With the anticipated driver shortage, the performance of employees in safety, personnel, and insurance could be extremely important to your company's ability to attract employees from a limited supply of workers. It is this department that sets the work atmosphere and conditions of employment.

In a driver shortage, the drivers can select the company they want to work for. If your company does not have a good reputation, you will have a hard time attracting the kinds of employees you need to succeed.

7

Data Processing Careers in Trucking

A data processing career in trucking can provide a very exciting challenge for a person who has an interest in computers and wants to be associated with an industry in which the computer is imperative for its survival.

Computers were introduced to the trucking industry in the early 1960s. At that time, the larger companies needed help with the large volumes of information they needed to process and store. While the record-keeping part of the computer function is still important, the use of the computer as a decision-making tool has become even more important to the industry.

Virtually every trucking company has some type of computer to assist in administrative functions. Even some independent owner-operators with a single-truck operation use a personal computer to keep records and determine if the freight they are hauling is generating a profit or costing them money.

In the larger companies, a central computer in the home office is used to link up the entire system, whether it comprises 5, 25, or 250 freight terminals. Each location has its own computer, which ties into the central computer via telephone lines. As a result, a company president can communicate with all of his or her terminal managers instantaneously. By the same token, each terminal can contact the home office or any other terminal in the field.

How It Works

Most companies have their payroll, dispatching, accounts payable and receivable, tracing, billing, and rating functions on the computer. An example of how one of these functions might work is the rating of a freight bill. A terminal in St. Paul, Minnesota might pick up a shipment to be delivered in Cleveland, Ohio the following morning. A clerk at the St. Paul terminal uses the computer to relay the information about the shipment to the home office, such as size, weight, number of pieces, and the commodity being shipped. A rater in the home office (a position covered in chapter 8) uses that information along with the classification for that commodity and the miles to be traveled to determine how much the company will charge for transporting the shipment. When the computer has calculated the information, the computer printer at the Cleveland terminal prints out a freight bill to accompany the shipment when it is delivered.

With information about the shipment, what trailer it is being shipped in, and dispatch information all fed into the computer, either the shipper or the receiver of the goods can determine almost instantly where the shipment is and when it will arrive at its destination. Many of the larger shippers have computers that tie into the computers of the trucking companies they use most. Those without a computer link can get the information almost as fast by calling the local terminal and asking the customer service representative to trace the shipment.

In addition to central computers, many trucking executives have a personal computer in their office to help in management functions. An example of one of

A data control clerk makes sure the information fed into the computer is accurate and adequate to achieve a particular data processing function.

these management functions is assessing the cost of freight. A sales executive might be in a customer's office soliciting business. The customer has some freight that could be handled by the company, but wants a special rate. With a telephone call to the home office, the sales executive gives management officials some basic facts about the type of freight, size, and destination. By feeding this information into the computer, along with software that contains information about labor, fuel, and equipment costs, it can quickly be determined if the freight can be handled at the desired rate and still generate a profit for the company. In such a competitive industry, it is vital to be able to assess the cost of freight quickly. Hauling freight that costs money to handle can put a company out of business in a hurry.

The computer operator has a vital role in the data processing necessary to keep the modern trucking company in operation.

With this basic understanding of a few of the many computer functions in the trucking industry, let's take a look at some of the data processing positions and careers that are available. It should be noted that in addition to full-time data processing positions, almost everyone in an administrative or management position needs basic computer knowledge. Some 80 to 85 percent of administrative or management people in trucking have daily contact with some computer function or printout.

SYSTEMS ANALYST

The systems analyst has the front-line contact with a potential user. The user tells the systems analyst his or her requirements. The systems analyst determines how to put together a program that best fits the user's needs. The systems analyst needs a basic knowledge of programming languages and knowledge of the trucking industry. A computer degree or a business administration degree with computer and transportation courses is desirable. An annual salary range of $33,000 to $38,000 can be expected.

PROGRAM ANALYST

Another important data processing position is that of the program analyst. The program analyst understands the program technology necessary to write the instructions for the use of the program or software. He or she works with the systems analyst in helping to meet the user's need. Salary averages $18,000 to $24,000. A degree in programming is desired.

DATA CONTROL CLERK

A data control clerk enters information into the computer. He or she also gathers computer printouts and gets them to the user. The educational requirement for this position is a high school diploma, with an emphasis on computer and data processing courses. The average salary is between $14,000 and $18,000.

COMPUTER OPERATOR

Another important data processing position is that of the computer operator, who runs the computer and must understand its technical functions.

Jerry

Jerry is a computer operator who has been running computers for the past twelve years, ten of them for a trucking company.

While the computer he now operates is similar to the one he operated in another industry, he says that the trucking position provides additional challenges since he has a central computer in addition to computer terminals at each of eighty freight terminals, all connected by telephone lines. He finds the work more interesting because he has an opportunity to work with the people at all the freight terminals as well as those in the home office data processing department. He says you have to like working with people and be able to handle pressure to be comfortable in this position. Jerry handles both quite well, but he finds shift work the biggest negative in his job. Despite that, he is happy with his decision to find a career in computers.

Using his free time for continuing education, Jerry hopes to move into computer management with his present employer.

An annual salary range of $16,000 to $21,000 can be expected in the computer operator position. An associate degree from a technical school is a necessity.

SYSTEMS PROGRAMMER

A systems programmer is employed to maintain the computer software. This position is becoming increasingly important as more programs become available and more functions are placed on the computer. A computer degree is required. The position has a salary range of $25,000 to $38,000.

DATABASE MANAGER

A database manager with a technical computer degree is employed to coordinate the information that will be used in the program. This person controls the database and ensures that the information used in the programming process is accurate. An annual salary of $20,000 to $24,000 can be expected.

PERSONAL COMPUTER COORDINATOR

The large trucking companies that use a number of personal computers employ a personal computer coordinator. This person selects computer hardware and software to ensure company-wide uniformity in the type of equipment and programs used. He or she earns an average salary of $18,000 to $24,000 by eliminating costly duplication and by ensuring that programs acquired for various managers are interchangeable. A technical degree is desired.

TELEPROCESSING COORDINATOR

Trucking companies with freight terminals in many cities must rely on telephone lines to network their system into a central computer. A teleprocessing coordinator seeks the best available and most cost-effective lines for communication. This person with a technical degree commands an annual salary of $18,000 to $24,000.

The actual job titles and even some of the work descriptions in data processing can vary from company to company. This chapter gives you an overall industry view, for the most part describing entry-level positions.

Certain important things should be remembered for those desiring a data processing career in trucking. First, it is not a nine-to-five job. The computer runs twenty-four hours a day, seven days a week, and you can expect shift work.

You will also be working closely with administrative and management officials and in some cases with customers. Therefore, it is important to be able to handle pressure and to enjoy working with people if you want a trucking data processing career.

It should be noted that the data processing people are located in the company's home office. So, depending on which trucking company you work for, you may have to relocate.

Because trucking knowledge along with computer knowledge is very important for a good industry data processing department, you gain excellent employment potential after you have held that first job in the industry.

If you are interested in the data processing field, and you possess the qualifications for the various positions described, you should submit your résumé to the director of management and information systems or someone with a similar title at the trucking companies where you would like to be employed.

A sample curriculum for a data processing technical school training program is listed in Appendix I.

The Future

Without a doubt, computers and the data processing people who operate those computers become more important to the trucking industry each day.

As an employee in the data processing department, you will constantly be providing management with key information. Your ability to get the computers and computer programs to play a more important role in the operation of your company will also result in a more important role for you in the company. For many it could lead to a management position. In any event, you will have a vital role in the operation of your company, and management will depend on you to help the company operate more smoothly and efficiently.

8

Traffic

The traffic department, which makes up about 10 percent of the general office staff of many trucking companies, has changed drastically since 1980 when economic deregulation was first introduced to the industry. Before then, uniform pricing by regional rate bureaus required none of the pricing and market analysis duties that now make the traffic department a key part of a successful carrier team.

Earlier you learned about the importance of pricing freight and establishing rates to make a carrier competitive in the marketplace, while generating enough profit to make the handling of the freight worth the company's effort. The research and analysis needed to write the programs that make it possible for the computer to provide accurate pricing information is one of the functions of the traffic department.

The senior members of the traffic department also become involved in customer negotiations, especially in national accounts where the corporate headquarters of a large manufacturing company select the carriers that will serve all its plant facilities around the country. Those decisions are usually based on bids submitted by the carriers. To submit an accurate bid, however, the traffic department has to meet with the customer to determine his or her exact needs. A customer may have very flexible service requirements, which should result

Traffic department raters make sure that the freight their company moves is billed accurately, so the maximum amount of revenue can be generated for the company.

in a more favorable freight rate. On the other hand, if a customer is attempting to run a production line from rolling truck deliveries, precise delivery times must be met and extra labor costs are incurred, justifying a higher bid by the carrier.

The traffic department also maintains one of its earlier functions of rating freight bills.

RATE CLERK

The rate clerk is the only truly entry-level position available in the traffic department. A person seeking a job as a rate clerk needs to be interested in working closely with a computer and be able to produce accurate work under pressure.

The rate clerk is expected to rate a large number of freight bills, with the assistance of a computer. The computer rating function was described in chapter 7. You will recall from that example that the freight is picked up in the daytime and the bills are rated at night so that they are ready for delivery with the freight the following morning. The night work is a factor that sometimes discourages a prospective employee, although some people like it. The opportunity for promotion to a day shift in the traffic department usually provides substantial motivation for rate clerks.

Joan

Joan, who has been rating freight bills since 1977, is a rating department supervisor. She looks forward to going to work each day because her job provides the challenges she feels make life interesting. She held other office jobs before becoming a rater, and she says she is very glad she made the career decision that gives her a key role in the trucking industry. According to Joan, her job is like a marathon race, and she always knows she is going to win. Each morning when the rating is completed for the day and the accurate bills are ready to start bringing in the revenue, Joan feels the race has been won.

Joan believes that raters play a very important role in the company's profit picture; by the production of accurate freight bills, the company gets the maximum revenue for the service it provides.

Joan says that the industry is made up of very nice people, and that the various rating departments she has worked in have usually had a strong team spirit. She says that those who have become quality industry raters would also be successful in almost any career effort they might consider. For Joan, rating is the right career choice.

Generally, a new rate clerk goes through a one-year training period before he or she achieves the speed and accuracy necessary to be of benefit to the employer. Accuracy is absolutely essential; inaccurate bills mean that either you are losing revenue for your company or you are overcharging the customer. Neither situation can continue to exist in a successful company. A good rate clerk achieves better than 98 percent accuracy. The minimum educational requirement for a rate clerk is a high school diploma; those wishing to advance should obtain a degree in transportation or physical distribution. A salary range of $18,000 to $25,000 can be expected.

TRANSPORTATION PRICING ANALYST

Transportation pricing analyst is a position of growing importance as more shippers opt for custom-designed rates and shipping contracts in the deregulated trucking industry. The transportation pricing analyst audits rate bills for accuracy and designs and publishes pricing packages to meet customers' needs. Analyzing competitive pricing packages and determining the company's ability to operate profitably are key functions in this new trucking era.

A transportation pricing analyst needs at least five years of rating experience. A technical school degree or a college degree in transportation marketing and physical distribution is a plus. The average annual salary for a transportation pricing analyst ranges between $25,000 and $30,000.

A career in a modern trucking company traffic department can indeed be exciting for an innovative person who likes to make things happen. With the competitive nature of the industry, innovation is often a necessary part of success. For instance, innovation in a traffic department can result in helping a manufacturing company get into new markets. Let's look at an East Coast manufacturer of paint that is seeking new markets in the Midwest.

The Midwest already has its own paint factories, which have a price advantage in the market because they don't have those long-distance shipping costs. However, a trucking company with an innovative traffic department is looking for freight coming from the East Coast to balance some shipments they have going to the East Coast. If, however, they have no freight to carry back on the return trip, which means no revenue to earn, the traffic department can offer a very reasonable rate to the eastern paint factory to get its product to the Midwest. This helps the trucking company compensate from what could have been nonrevenue-producing miles. The negotiations between the trucking company and the factory's shipping department can also lead to the carrier transporting more of the factory's freight to other areas.

Those interested in analysis and marketing can find an exciting challenge in helping to keep the American economy growing and moving through a career in a trucking company traffic department.

The experience gained in a trucking company's traffic department can also be used in a transfer to the traffic department of a manufacturing firm that purchases service from trucking companies. Obviously, the knowledge of what trucking companies can do for a shipper and what goes into those negotiations can be valuable when you are on the other side of the fence purchasing that service.

9

Accounting

The general accounting department of most trucking companies is responsible for preparing financial statements, corporate taxes, and financial forecasts, and for coordinating internal and external audits.

ACCOUNTANT

Accountant is the entry-level position for the general accounting department of a trucking company. Depending on the size of the company, the accountant may specialize in taxes, financial forecasting, or one of the other functions mentioned. In smaller companies, all of those functions may be handled by one person.

A trucking industry accountant should have a college degree in accounting. He or she must be well organized and have an appreciation for details. The ability to work well with people is especially important, since terminal managers as well as people in the home office are involved in compiling the information needed to do the job.

Most accountants find additional challenges in the trucking industry, one of them being cost accounting. In manufacturing industries it is relatively simple to use proven accounting practices to determine the cost of a particular product. In trucking, coming up with an accurate cost for the service sold can be extremely challenging, as shipments differ widely. They require different kinds of handling or different amounts of time to pick up or deliver depending on where the shipper and the receiver are located. The number of stop signs en route, traffic jams, and other intangible factors all play a role in the actual cost, and often those costs can vary from one day to the next.

Financial forecasting can present its own unique challenge in this industry. While all financial forecasting has some element of risk, because the forecasts are based on anticipated economic projections, the trucking industry is dependent on all of the various industries for its revenue-producing services.

Trucking industry accountants are entry-level positions averaging about $18,000 annually.

The successful accountant can look forward to promotion to the positions of controller and vice president of finance when his or her experience and work history correspond with an opening in those positions.

REVENUE ACCOUNTING

An industry revenue accounting department handles the credit and collection management functions. A college degree and experience in the other positions covered in this chapter are prerequisites for becoming a director of this department.

CREDIT-COLLECTION MANAGER

The industry credit-collection manager usually establishes the guidelines, does research, and monitors the progress of collections. The position requires a person who can work well under pressure, has good writing and oral communication skills, and can convert a sometimes embarrassing situation with a customer into a company plus. Timely decision-making and diplomacy are musts. As an example of the delicate situations that might arise, suppose a large customer starts having financial problems and falling behind in the payment of freight bills. You are faced with the options of cutting off credit to that customer and risking the loss of the entire account, or letting the customer slip further behind and risking a loss of thousands of dollars for the company should the customer face ultimate bankruptcy.

The credit manager also works closely with terminal salespeople to make sure they make collections before customers get too far behind in payments.

Qualifications for this position are a college degree in business and some experience in the industry. The salary range is between $25,000 and $30,000.

The credit manager must also have some public relations skills. As society relies more on credit, the credit manager has to determine when the customer is using trucking company money.

Often shippers that are able to pay their freight bills delay as long as possible so that their money can continue to draw interest while they use your company's money.

If you allow this to continue, your company will have to increase its line of credit and pay more interest. A great deal of tact must be used when attempting to end such a practice, or you risk losing that shipper to your competition.

On the other hand, with the high cost of interest and the close margins under which some trucking companies operate, you may have to decide when your company is better off without that particular shipper's business.

SUPERVISOR OF BILLS

The supervisor of bills is the entry-level position for the revenue accounting department. He or she assists the credit-collections manager in performing the duties described above.

An associate degree in business is the minimum educational requirement and a four-year degree can help with later promotions.

A salary range of $18,000 to $25,000 is the industry average.

Payroll

Accurate paychecks that keep employees happy is the mission of the payroll department of most trucking companies. Those paychecks go out weekly in the trucking industry, rather than twice monthly as is standard practice in many other industries.

The payroll staff, which consists of payroll clerks and supervisors, has to deal with several methods of pay. In most companies, over-the-road drivers are paid by the mile. However, they may also receive hourly wages for time spent hooking up equipment, or time spent dropping off shipments en route to a final destination. The payroll clerk studies trip reports to obtain the necessary information to feed into a computer, which ultimately calculates the pay and prints the check.

In addition to the miles/hourly combination checks for over-the-road drivers, checks must be calculated for local drivers, maintenance employees, and other hourly employees.

Persons interested in a payroll clerk position should have either a technical school or college degree in accounting and have great concern for accuracy. Inaccurate checks can lead to conflict, and the payroll clerk is usually the person employees go to if they feel there are mistakes in their checks. So in addition to accuracy, a payroll clerk must have the ability to communicate and work well with people.

Because the computer is used in calculating the payroll, the payroll department is generally kept quite lean. This factor makes it essential for those seeking payroll clerk positions to be dependable, with a work history that does not include absenteeism.

Payroll employees can play an important role in how the company is viewed by its drivers. With the predicted driver shortage, that is crucial to the company's ability to attract and keep drivers.

One of the worst human relations mistakes a company can make is to inflict payroll delays or mistakes on its employees.

The payroll clerk's annual salary range is between $18,000 and $25,000.

10

Claims, Claim Prevention, Security

The handling of claims for lost or damaged freight, claim prevention, and security are duties that generally fall under one department in the home office of most trucking companies.

CLAIM AGENT

If a customer's freight is lost or damaged while it is being handled by a carrier, the claim must be adjusted much in the same way an insurance claim is resolved, or the customer might stop doing business with that carrier. However, the claim agent must also consider what is fair for the carrier and not overpay just to keep the customer happy. Not every case of damage is the fault of the carrier.

Claim agent is seldom an entry-level job. Usually some terminal experience as a customer service representative is necessary. A great deal of verifying paperwork must accompany a claim, and claim agents must be familiar with tariff and bill of lading terms and conditions.

Since working with the customer filing a claim is necessary, a pleasant personality that presents your company in its best light during an unpleasant situation is a quality required for a good claim agent. Writing, oral, and communication skills are also important. If an

Claim prevention is enhanced by periodic checks of loading and packaging practices.

agreement cannot be reached between you and the customer, you may also have to represent your company in court.

If one of your company's trucks becomes involved in an accident, you would probably be called to the scene of the accident, especially if there appeared to be freight damage. You may be called out at all hours of the day or night and should not count on a nine-to-five job.

89

The various demands of the job make clear why the background in service representative work is desired. A high school diploma is essential, and some college work in law or business law is very helpful. The salary range is $18,000 to $25,000.

CLAIM PREVENTION

If settling a claim can help customer relations, preventing a claim will do even more for the positive relationship trucking companies would like to have with their customers. The claim prevention specialist works closely with those who handle the freight in an effort to prevent loss and damage.

A claim prevention agent is experienced in freight handling and has probably served as a customer service representative or in some other capacity in which he or she became familiar with freight-handling techniques. The promotion of claim-prevention contests, editing of claim-prevention brochures and posters, and making of training tapes and films are all part of the job. In addition, he or she attends safety meetings and other training sessions.

When special problems arise with a shipper's freight, the claim prevention specialist might meet with the customer in an attempt to devise some packaging or handling method to solve the difficulty.

A candidate for such a position should have some teaching skills and the ability to work well with people. Success or failure on the job depends on how well he or she can motivate others to follow programs and instructions that will prevent freight loss or damage.

A trucking company's ability to operate with minimal losses or damages is almost always featured in its marketing efforts. Even though a customer may recover the losses that result from damaged freight, most customers would prefer never seeing a claim. The receiver of the freight is the shipper's customer, and that receiver may need the product immediately, so there is little consolation in knowing that the damaged goods will be replaced or the cost will be covered by the carrier. The end receiver tends to associate the quality of his or her supplier with the condition of the product when it arrives. For that reason most quality-conscious shippers seek carriers that provide claim-free service.

As was said earlier, claim prevention specialist is not an entry-level position. Depending on the size of the company, the job pays an annual salary of $30,000 to $40,000.

HAZARDOUS MATERIALS

Among the major new concerns for claims officials in recent years are the new hazardous materials laws. These laws are intended to protect the public, but they can result in stiff penalties for your company if they are not carefully followed.

The laws require proper identification on trucks when hazardous materials are being carried. They also require special actions in cases when a container is damaged and leaks hazardous material on the highway.

After you accept a claims position, becoming familiar with the hazardous materials regulations should be one of your early priorities.

SECURITY

Because of the nature of the business, security is crucial to the success of a trucking company. Many companies shy away from extremely valuable freight because of the danger of theft. Just one major loss could cost the company more than all the revenue that account might generate for several years. Although avoiding extremely high-value freight reduces the risk, all freight has some

91

value and the carrier must accept some risk to stay in business.

Most trucking companies protect themselves by employing state-of-the-art security systems.

DIRECTOR OF SECURITY SYSTEMS

The trucking industry offers several security positions for a person interested in law enforcement. The larger carriers employ first-rate people they recruit from police and sheriff departments or even the Federal Bureau of Investigation (FBI). This director of security systems is well paid and oversees the security for a company's entire system, which may include several hundred terminal facilities. Substantial travel may be included in the position. In addition to law enforcement experience, a candidate for this position should have some type of degree in law enforcement or police science.

SECURITY GUARD

The second security position is that of a security guard who physically keeps an eye on a particular facility. These positions are generally filled by people with security guard or police backgrounds. Often they are filled by off-duty police officers. The compensation generally varies with the size of the city. In many instances a guard service is employed, and the guards are employed by the service rather than the trucking company.

11

Communications and Public Affairs

The need to communicate with a number of different audiences has resulted in a new position at most of the larger trucking companies. Most communications, public affairs, or public relations departments have been established within the past fifteen years. Public relations is a concept that is relatively new to the industry because of the way companies are established and grow in the trucking industry. Most companies started as a family operation; as they needed more capacity to meet customers' needs, more trucks and more people were added. Public relations and governmental affairs were largely left to the American Trucking Associations and the various state associations. Today, many company chief executives realize that they must communicate with a number of groups on a company level.

Employees
Probably the most important of these groups is the company's employees. Newsletters and company newspapers are the most common form of internal communication. Video technology has also made it possible for companies to produce their own training tapes and use

this audiovisual medium to communicate company goals and methods for accomplishing certain functions. Slide presentations and the writing of speeches are other internal public relations functions.

Customers
Communication with customers is another very important function of a modern trucking company. This is generally done by advertising in trade publications or issuing press releases to the various magazines and newspapers that might reach the customer. Innovation is very important in the customer relations effort. The public relations employee with new ideas can be a valuable asset to the company.

Community
Public affairs officers in the trucking industry may also become involved in community relations in the various communities the company serves. News releases to newspapers and radio and television stations are only one form of community relations. Others are participation in community projects, such as the United Way, chamber of commerce activities, and presentations at school career days. Community relations might also involve crisis management duties if a company truck should become involved in a serious accident. This would be especially true if hazardous materials were involved in the accident or if some other life-threatening situation resulted.

Investors
Publicly held companies have an audience they need to reach, and this is accomplished through investor relations. Annual and quarterly reports and media releases are among the basic functions in the investor relations area. The organization of the annual shareholder

meeting is also a function of the public relations department in a publicly held company.

Government

Many trucking companies are becoming involved in governmental affairs in various ways. Some have organized political action committees to raise funds for the campaigns of candidates who are favorable to legislative positions that the industry support. There are also educational efforts, such as letter-writing campaigns. One of the newer approaches is arranging legislative visits to trucking company facilities where the senator or congressperson can meet with people in the industry. He or she can also ride in a truck with a driver and see the products manufactured by community industries that need a good transportation system to get those goods to market and keep the local voters employed. The pressure of taxes on the industry and other legislative matters that affect trucking companies make governmental affairs a high priority for most carriers.

The company's public affairs director usually works closely with the efforts and campaigns of the state and national associations so that a unified image can be projected for the entire trucking industry.

Most public affairs staffs are small. In many cases one person may be responsible for all of the duties described. A person seeking such a position should be interested in hard work and love to meet and work with people. Substantial travel may be part of the job; the company may have terminal facilities across the country, and personal contact with the employees is necessary to do the job right. The person would also have the opportunity to ride in the trucks while interviewing drivers for articles to be used in the company newspaper or in a public release.

Meeting Planning

Sales meetings, training sessions, and customer appreciation functions are often included in the duties of the public relations coordinator.

In each of these areas, innovation is probably the most important contribution that can be made. Many people are overexposed to sales meetings, training sessions, and other motivational efforts; therefore, a successful function must be well planned, with a unique theme.

The same is true for customer relations efforts. The coordinator is in fact competing for time with other companies. Success in making functions distinctly different, but enjoyable, will create a good impression for the company. Planning and organization are very important. If customers receive good impressions from the function, they will think highly of the company.

Qualifications

The position of public affairs director is filled with excitement and challenge. A college degree in journalism or public affairs is desirable. Some entry-level positions exist, but most public affairs staffs are small, and the companies prefer to hire someone with experience as a newspaper or broadcast reporter or from a public relations company. Skills desirable for such a position include the ability to write news releases and speeches, to edit newspapers, to use a camera and all types of audiovisual equipment, and to speak effectively. An understanding of the political process is also beneficial.

The salary for such a position varies greatly depending on the duties, the size of the company, and the candidate's experience. An entry-level salary of $18,000 and up could be expected.

12

General Office

Usually headed by a manager, the general office department has functions that vary greatly depending on the size of the trucking company.

In addition to fulfilling the needs and requests of the various departments and terminals in the system, the functions of purchasing, clerical, and filing can also be covered by the general office staff.

The general office manager is usually an experienced trucking company employee who excels in office procedures and possesses the skills to interview and employ competent office and clerical employees.

Probably one of the most important functions of this department is the coordinating and purchasing of office equipment, supplies, even furniture, and anything that enables the entire company to run as a smooth unit.

The general office department has excellent entry-level opportunities for those interested in a trucking career. One need not be confined to the home office. Once a person understands a particular company's operation, terminal positions can also be secured by the ambitious employee.

Entry-level employees with clerical skills are generally hired to perform filing, typing, bookkeeping, word processing, and clerical functions. The qualifications may vary, but a well-rounded clerical education at a technical school should provide the necessary skills for

Proficiency on various business and office machines is important for an individual seeking a general office position in the modern trucking industry.

such a position. Specialization in areas, such as word processing, stenography, and business machines, can increase employability. Sample technical school curricula that would prepare you for a position in the general office department are listed in Appendix I.

Accuracy is very important to any of these functions, and for a person seeking such a position, attention to detail and accuracy are important. The ability to work with other people is always important in this people-oriented business that requires teamwork for success.

The salary for entry-level people in clerical positions ranges from $6 to $12 per hour.

The potential for advancement and movement into other departments in the trucking industry is very good for the aggressive person who will seek out new opportunities and obtain the appropriate education. While the functions of the general office department are key and vital to the smooth operation of any trucking company, they can also serve as a proving ground for those interested in promotion and advancement.

As in many of the other positions discussed, the ability to show an interest in the customer and generate new business for the company is very important. A sincere interest in the success of the company should allow you opportunities to apply for advanced positions with better salaries.

13

Is Trucking the Right Career for You?

Having reviewed the various career options in the trucking industry, you now have the opportunity to decide if one of those career choices is for you.

The salaries alone may be a temptation for young people considering their futures. Keep in mind that the salaries given are only industry averages. The actual pay you might receive from a given employer could vary widely, depending on your experience, the region of the country, the size of the operation, and whether the company is union or nonunion. Many of the new companies entering the industry are nonunion carriers and, in most cases, the salaries they pay could be at the low end of the averages. At present, more openings are probably available with these new carriers. Depending on inflation and other factors, salaries could change dramatically. The average salaries given should, however, provide some measure of the benefits of trucking compared to other careers.

Although salaries are important considerations in making a career choice, other factors are equally important. Ultimately you will be happy and fulfilled only if the job you pick provides you with the challenges and working conditions that make you want to get up and go to work each day. Each of the positions discussed probably has some disadvantages along with the advantages. The disadvantages should be carefully weighed before making that career choice.

You should also carefully consider the personality types needed for the various positions. Trucking is a people business, and in almost every case the job calls for a person with an outgoing personality who enjoys being with and working with other people.

Because trucking is a service industry, it is also very demanding, with substantial pressure existing in most of the positions listed. In this day and age, customers demand fast, dependable service, and only people who thrive on pressure and challenges can really enjoy many of the positions the industry has to offer.

You will be expected to be a team player, and you will find that trucking companies are only as good as their weakest workers. The best efforts made in St. Louis, Missouri to provide service to a receiver of goods in Dallas, Texas will do little good if the Dallas crew doesn't follow through with prompt handling of the shipment when it arrives.

The teamwork concept is also very important among the different positions in a company. As you read about the various positions, you probably noticed that words like vital, key, and essential were constantly used in describing them. That is not just a matter of overemphasizing the importance of each position; they are, in fact, all key and vital to the success of a carrier. The best drivers in the world won't be working very long if the sales force doesn't secure enough freight to keep them busy. An outstanding sales force cannot be successful if the operations end doesn't provide the quality of service that the customer wants and needs. The best operations efforts can move the freight only if the maintenance department keeps the equipment in good operating condition. The best-maintained equipment can move only if safety and insurance do their part to establish a good safety record so insurance can be obtained to cover that equipment while freight is being moved. Those are just a few examples of the importance of teamwork in the trucking industry. That interdependence can be seen in claim prevention, data processing, traffic, or any other function in the industry.

14

Finding That First Job

The trucking industry is like other industries when it comes to finding that first job. Everybody seems to be looking for employees with some experience. But how do you get the experience you need if you can't get a job that will provide it? Well, it's not as hopeless as it might sound. There are companies that will hire promising young people even without experience. That first job may have to be with one of the smaller companies, but once you have experience you can pick the job you want—and it may well be with that same small company. Aggressive, small companies grow, and if your determination, dedication, and innovation play a role in that growth, you will probably be very happy and fulfilled with your position in the company.

There are also other ways of getting that industry experience. Many companies hire high school students for part-time office help. That position may not be the trucking career you are thinking about, but the experience may open some doors to you when you apply for the position of your choice.

It should be noted that the U.S. military has positions for truck drivers, diesel mechanics, data processing and computer experts, and others that provide experience that can help in your trucking career. The military is an option for those seeking experience, and it is one that eliminates the educational costs that might be necessary with some other options. It could be especially beneficial for the young person having difficulty coming up with the funds necessary for training in a civilian school.

Knowledge is power when you go for that first job interview. Before you file your résumé with a company, take a little time to do some research and get some information about the company. If it is a publicly held company, you could study its annual report. By writing to the company you can probably obtain a company history or other information that could help you. Anything that can give you an edge when you are applying for a position is helpful.

Customer information is also very important. Watch for the company's trucks around town. When you see them at the loading docks of businesses and industries where you have a contact, get that contact to introduce you to officials in the shipping department. Any customer information you have when you go for your interview is bound to serve you well: Trucking companies are in business to serve their customers.

You may also need to know how to find trucking companies. Most people would be surprised to learn how many trucking companies serve even the smaller communities. If your city is not the home office of a trucking company, you probably have heard very little about it. Most trucking companies maintain a low profile other than with potential customers. Their terminals are probably not in the most visible locations, and they may be forbidding in appearance. Do not let that discourage you from seeking employment with a particular carrier. The company might have 100 terminals around the country, some very large and modern and some that serve only a small area. The terminal facility often has little to do with working conditions, salaries, or how successful a particular carrier might be. The best way

Dump trucks are familiar scenes at quarries and all types of construction sites.

to find out how many trucking companies and prospective employers your city has is to check the yellow pages for a full listing.

Finally, when searching for a career in trucking, don't limit your search to those listed as for-hire trucking companies. Your city has many businesses and industries that employ truck drivers, diesel mechanics, dispatchers, and other positions covered in this book, but they are not listed as trucking companies. They include factories that have a private fleet of trucks, bakeries, milk bottling firms, petroleum and petrochemical companies with tank fleets, concrete companies, lumber companies, meat packaging firms, vegetable farms, furniture stores, and an almost endless list of others. All of

105

these various firms can provide excellent first-job experience for those determined to have a career in trucking. The salaries may be substantially below those mentioned earlier, but the experience may be the ticket you need for your desired career in trucking.

Making the Best Impression

It would be impossible to describe the perfect employee; however, there are a number of qualities that employers in the competitive trucking industry are seeking. It should be noted, of course, that those doing the hiring are human beings with individual personalities and preferences. The composite ideal employee described in the next few pages has qualities that you might emulate to help you score important points during your interview.

Appearance

Appearance is obviously important in any job interview. It is, however, especially important in a service industry, such as trucking, where so many employees have direct contact with the customer.

The ideal applicant reports to the job interview in clean, neat clothing. Obviously, the style of clothes would vary depending on the position you want. An applicant for a sales position or a management training position would make the best impression in a blue or gray suit with a modest tie or a conservative dress, but a driver might well make the best impression in a fresh work uniform or a clean shirt and blue jeans. Leaning to the conservative and avoiding bright or flashy clothes is almost always the best choice. Another suggestion is leaving your cowboy hat or boots at home. Although the industry is often associated with the country western style, there is a concerted effort to change its image and get rid of the cowboy look. If your interviewer favors the image change, you will score much higher without the hat or boots.

The interviewer is interested in more than the clothing you wear to the interview. He or she will try to judge what kind of clothing you will wear on the job. This is extremely important because customers choose the carrier that best serves to enhance their product's image. When you pick up freight at a customer's place of business or make a sales call, the customer will be drawing conclusions about the company based on your appearance. A driver in an unkempt t-shirt and a pair of dirty jeans is not going to give an impression of a quality operation to a waiting customer. By the same token, a bright or loud sports jacket may not create the professional sales image many customers desire. The customer wants his or her product to be the best in quality and appearance. Therefore he or she will do business with carriers whose people look like winners and enhance his or her product image. Those making employment decisions for trucking companies will be looking to hire winners.

Still on the subject of appearance, for men a well-groomed beard or mustache may be acceptable to most interviewers; however, the clean-shaven look with a neat haircut will give you an edge in most instances.

Even the car you drive to the interview can be a factor. That does not mean you need to go out and rent or purchase an expensive car. But if the interviewer can hear you coming two blocks away, or if the dents and rust on your car make it look as if it might have to be towed away, you may want to borrow a friend's car. The person doing the hiring is looking for a winner to help make his or her employee team more impressive to the customer; don't let the interviewer think that you are not a desirable employee because of what you drive.

Personality

The trucking industry is extremely competitive. Those hiring employees are looking for positive, happy, enthusiastic people with infectious, optimistic attitudes.

The positive, happy type of person is very important to the interviewer because trucking is truly a people business. When hiring a manager, the interviewer will be looking for a person who can transmit that positive attitude to his or her staff. When hiring a dispatcher or customer service clerk, the interviewer will be looking for a positive, pleasant person who will transmit professionalism over the telephone to the customer. When hiring a driver who makes pickups at the customer's dock, the interviewer will be looking for a driver with a personality that makes him or her a welcome visitor. The more the customers like a driver, the more shipments they are going to send via that particular carrier. On the other hand, if a driver is rude, grumpy, or just gives the impression that the customer should be grateful he or she is there to pick up the freight, the customer may decide to use another carrier with a more pleasant driver.

Projecting the Proper Safety Attitude

Keeping a spotless driving record from the day you obtain your driver's license is very important. The importance of this safety factor for anyone desiring a career as a professional driver cannot be overemphasized.

Trucking companies make a substantial investment in equipment. They are not going to entrust that equipment to anyone who cannot even handle a car without being involved in accidents or traffic violations.

You will certainly be asked about your driving record during an interview for a professional driving position. Even if you desire a position that does not involve driving a company vehicle, if you can suggest to the interviewer that you are genuinely interested in safety and promoting safety, it will be important in securing the job. The amount of money a carrier invests in equipment, the increasing cost of insurance, and the customers' desire to use a carrier that gets their products to the destination safely are all of vital importance to any trucking company. Anything you can do to show your shared concern for safety will score interview points for you.

Job Versus Career

Because of the good salaries that are associated with trucking industry positions, there is usually little difficulty in finding job applicants. But in this new competitive era, there is not much need for someone looking for just a job. What the interviewer will be looking for is an applicant looking for a career. There is a difference. One who seeks a career generally makes more of a commitment to seeing his or her firm be successful. That commitment will translate into concern for the customer in an effort to help the company grow and be well regarded. That commitment will also show in the quality of work. An employee with a career commitment will be looking for advancement. He or she will perform in a manner that will benefit the company, so the advancement will follow.

A career-minded employee will also be interested in seeing the company be profitable. Profit is an absolute must for any company desiring to stay in business. Your understanding of the importance of profit and your ability to show that interest during the interview will score points for you.

Team Player

The importance of teamwork to the success of a company has been discussed several times in this book.

109

It is therefore appropriate to remind you in this chapter that the interviewer will be looking for team players. If you aren't a team player, all your other good qualities may be of little value. Displaying team-player skills during a job interview may not be easy, but you can expect the interviewer to be watching for signs indicating how much interest you have in other people and the operation as a whole.

Be Genuine

It is very important during the interview for you to accentuate your strong points in each of the areas mentioned in this chapter. It is just as important that you don't go overboard. Most interviewers are experienced professionals who can spot phony claims. Remember also that in most new jobs you will have a probation period during which you will have an opportunity to prove all the claims you made about yourself and your abilities during your interview.

A job interview is your opportunity to sell yourself to the employer. If you do a good job of selling yourself, you may become an employee. If you fail to sell yourself you will continue to be a job seeker. A job interview is not the time to be modest. It is a time to be genuine, while emphasizing your skills and qualifications. Convince the interviewer of why you are the right person for the job.

15

New Technology and the Future

The trucking industry has been changing constantly since it was founded and it will continue to be in transition into the twenty-first century.

As mentioned earlier, improved computer technology and satellite communication play major roles in the industry. According to a survey of 700 fleets conducted by the ATA:

- 46 percent of motor carriers use mobile communications;
- 19 percent use a computer-aided dispatch or routing system;
- 10 percent use a computer in their trucks;
- 11 percent use electronic data exchange in business transactions.

This technology will continue to play a vital role in the future of trucking.

Rising fuel prices, concern for the environment, and the driver shortage are all factors under consideration in the design laboratories where the trucks of the future are being developed. Some changes are already showing up in the marketplace.

In an effort to attract and retain drivers, trucking companies are buying tractors with all the comforts of home. The manufacturers of this equipment keep coming up with new amenities.

While gear-jamming is part of the industry's macho image, trucks with automatic transmissions may be part of the answer to the driver shortage. Trucks with automatic transmissions are easier to drive and may attract more drivers. In some vocational trucking applications, such as waste management, trucks with automatic transmissions are already outselling the manual transmission units.

The concern for air quality in the major cities is prompting consideration of less polluting engines, such as a smokeless engine. Still others are saying that alternate fuel is the answer and the days of the diesel engine are numbered. Most people associated with trucking, however, feel that diesel is the only fuel that will generate the power necessary for the heavy loads that a trucking company needs to move to remain profitable.

Aerodynamic configurations and much longer combination vehicles could emerge to deal with both the energy crisis and the driver shortage.

The longer combination vehicles would allow a company to move much more freight with fewer drivers. In the past two decades the industry has moved from 45-foot to 53-foot trailers. Some are predicting combination 53-foot trailers for the future. That, however, would necessitate legislative changes to permit use of the larger vehicles on highways and interstates. At the present time, combination vehicles are allowed in most areas, but they are the substantially shorter 28-foot trailers.

The exact impact on the need for drivers will be determined by the success of the industry in changing the length and weight restrictions under which it must operate.

There are some certainties for the future employees of the trucking industry. The most important is job security for those employees and companies that can meet the challenges. Regardless of the ultimate outcome of deregulation, the need for trucks and the movement of freight will continue to grow as the country grows. To some extent, that growth will always be dependent on the nation's economy. However, even when Americans purchase imports, those imports have to be moved from the seaport to customers—via trucks.

The number of communities served exclusively by truck transportation grows each day. Over half of American cities have no other means of receiving goods or shipping out the products that they raise or manufacture.

"If you got it, a truck brought it." That slogan has been around since long before truck deregulation, but it is as true today as when it was first coined. The slogan indicates that job security is available to the dedicated trucking employee. The nationwide need for truck transportation ensures a future for the industry. The future of your company, however, is dependent on the performance the company gets from you and other members of your employee team.

Throughout this book emphasis has been placed on teamwork, dedication, quality work, service, and a concern for the customer. Those qualities are the future of the trucking industry. It's a future that can also be yours.

Appendix I

College degrees to qualify for various trucking positions can be earned in most of the public and private colleges and universities around the country. For some positions, however, post-high school training is obtained in a trade or technical school. Some of the trade schools trying to attract young people seeking high-paying jobs in the trucking industry have gained a reputation for being more interested in the tuition they collect than in the future of the young people who pay that tuition. That negative image should not be associated with all trade schools. Many do a fine job of serving an important need.

Young people must be careful, however, to check out a school before they make monetary commitments. You can do several things to protect yourself. You might start by checking with several trucking companies to see if your chances for employment with them would be enhanced by attending the school you are considering. You could also obtain a list of the school's recent graduates, talk to them, and find out if they are employed in positions they trained for and if that training helped them get their jobs.

You can also get help from your high school career or guidance counselor, who can help you check the curriculum offerings. In the following pages are listed the Proposed Minimum Standards for Training Tractor-Trailer Drivers as prepared by the Office of Motor Carriers, Federal Highway Administration, U.S. Department of Transportation.

The curriculum at a school you are considering may not be identical to the one given here, but the course of study should at least be comparable and provide similar amounts of actual behind-the-wheel driving experience. The good schools probably offer additional courses in customer relations and other related fields that would help you be a better employee in this competitive, people-oriented service industry.

Also listed are sample curricula for those interested in careers as trucking industry diesel mechanics, data processing employees, and general office employees. Again, the curriculum of the school of your choice may not be identical, but should be comparable. The samples are from technical schools that have trucking industry officials serving on their curriculum advisory committees.

GENERAL CURRICULUM STANDARDS

OVERVIEW

The General Curriculum Standards recommended by the Office of Motor Carriers provide a basic instructional program for training tractor-trailer drivers. This section contains an overview of the curriculum subjects; instructional sequence, objectives, and methods; and the minimum number of hours necessary for accomplishing the objectives of these Standards.

This curriculum is designed for students who are already licensed as automobile drivers. Therefore, many of the traditional subjects found in other driver training courses are not included.

ORGANIZATION

The curriculum is divided into sections, units, and lessons. Five sections of instruction are used, with each section containing from three to nine units, and each unit containing two or more lessons. In the five sections, a total of twenty-nine units and seventy-two lessons are presented.

Sections

Each section has different objectives:

Section 1: Basic Operation—This section covers the interaction between students and the vehicle. It is intended to teach students to control the motion of the vehicle, ensure it is in proper operating condition, and confirm that it is correctly coupled to trailers.

Section 2: Safe Operating Practices—This section covers the interaction between the student/vehicle combination and the highway traffic environment. It is intended to teach students to apply their basic operating skills in a way that ensures their own safety and that of other road users.

Section 3: Advanced Operating Practices—This section covers the higher level skills needed to cope with the hazards of the roadway traffic environment. Its purpose is to develop the perceptual skills needed to recognize a potential hazard, as well as the manipulative skills needed to handle the vehicle in an emergency.

Section 4: Vehicle Maintenance—This section covers the manner in which the various components of the vehicle work so students can recognize a malfunction or safety hazard before it causes serious damage or an accident. Its purpose is to teach students to perform routine service functions and simple maintenance tasks and to recognize when the vehicle needs repairs.

Section 5: Nonvehicle Activities—This section covers activities not directly related to the vehicle. Its purpose is to teach students to carry out these activities in a way that protects their safety and the safety of the vehicle, cargo, and other motorists.

Units and Lessons

A unit is a set of instructional activities, with the same instructional objectives, and is divided into lessons. The course outline that follows contains an overview of the twenty-nine units and seventy-two lessons. Lessons are divided into the following categories by the type of activity used to instruct students:

Classroom Lessons—Classroom instruction occurs indoors, accomplished by instructional aids that allow large numbers of students to be taught effectively at one time.

Lab Lessons—Laboratory instruction refers to any instruction occurring outside of a classroom that does not involve actual operation of the vehicle or its components. It may take place in a parking lot, garage, or facility owned by a dealer or fleet operator.

Range Lessons—Range instruction is instruction that occurs on a protected off-street "Driving Range," where students may make use of tractor-trailers without hazard from cars or other road users. Those schools that lack access to off-street facilities may

CURRICULUM UNIT STANDARDS OUTLINE

	Number of Lessons (Optional)	MINIMUM HOURS REQUIRED				
		Classroom	Lab	Range	Street	Total
SECTION 1—BASIC OPERATION						
Unit 1.1—Orientation	3	3.25	1.00	0	0	4.25
Unit 1.2—Control Systems	2	1.75	.75	0	0	2.50
Unit 1.3—Vehicle Inspection	2	2.00	4.00	0	0	6.00
Unit 1.4—Basic Control	4	.75	0	7.25	0	8.00
Unit 1.5—Shifting	2	1.25	0	3.00	0	4.25
Unit 1.6—Backing	2	.75	0	22.00	0	22.75
Unit 1.7—Coupling and Uncoupling	2	.75	0	3.50	0	4.25
Unit 1.8—Proficiency Development: Basic Control	3	1.50	0	36.00	18.00	55.50
Unit 1.9—Special Rigs	2	1.00	3.50*	0	0	4.50
TOTALS	22	13.00	9.25	71.75	18.00	112.00
SECTION 2—SAFE OPERATING PRACTICES						
Unit 2.1—Visual Search	3	1.25	.75	0	8.00	10.00
Unit 2.2—Communication	2	1.25	0	0	3.00	4.25
Unit 2.3—Speed Management	2	2.00	0	1.75	0	3.75
Unit 2.4—Space Management	2	1.75	0	0	6.00	7.75
Unit 2.5—Night Operation	3	.75	0	3.00	4.50	8.25
Unit 2.6—Extreme Driving Conditions	2	3.25	0	4.00	0	7.25
Unit 2.7—Proficiency Development: Safe Operating Procedures	2	1.00	0	0	70.50	71.50
TOTALS	16	11.25	.75	8.75	92.00	112.75

	Number of Lessons (Optional)	MINIMUM HOURS REQUIRED				
		Classroom	Lab	Range	Street	Total
SECTION 3—ADVANCED OPERATING PRACTICES						
Unit 3.1—Hazard Perception	2	1.50	0	0	6.00	7.50
Unit 3.2—Emergency Maneuvers	2	1.50	0	4.00	0	5.50
Unit 3.3—Skid Control and Recovery	2	1.25	0	7.75*	0	9.00
TOTALS	6	4.25	0	11.75	6.00	22.00
SECTION 4—VEHICLE MAINTENANCE						
Unit 4.1—Vehicle Systems	2	11.25	2.00	0	0	13.25
Unit 4.2—Preventive Maintenance and Servicing	4	1.25	7.50	0	0	8.75
Unit 4.3—Diagnosing and Reporting Malfunctions	2	3.00	1.00	0	0	4.00
TOTALS	8	15.50	10.50	0	0	26.00
SECTION 5—NONVEHICLE ACTIVITIES						
Unit 5.1—Handling Cargo	4	5.00	4.00*	0	0	9.00
Unit 5.2—Cargo Documentation	2	4.75	0	0	0	4.75
Unit 5.3—Hours of Service Requirements	3	5.75	0	0	0	5.75
Unit 5.4—Accident Procedures	4	13.00*	.75	0	0	13.75
Unit 5.5—Personal Health and Safety	3	5.00	0	0	0	5.00
Unit 5.6—Trip Planning	2	4.75	0	0	0	4.75
Unit 5.7—Public and Employer Relations	2	4.25*	0	0	0	4.25
TOTALS	20	42.50	4.75	0	0	47.25
TOTAL	72	86.50	25.25	92.25	116.00	320.00

29 Units (Mandatory) and 72 Lessons (Optional)
* = Portions of time are optional.

119

conduct range instruction on public property, provided adequate control of other traffic is available to avoid danger to students, instructors, or other road users.

Street Lessons—Street instruction refers to behind-the-wheel (BTW) instruction that occurs in roadway configurations and traffic conditions needed to satisfy the objectives of the lessons for which the instruction is required.

NOTE: No lesson involves more than a single mode.

COURSE OUTLINE
Section 1—Basic Operation

Purpose
To introduce students to curriculum components of the tractor-trailer and basic maneuvers.
At end of section, students will have acquired the skill and knowledge to operate a tractor-trailer combination well enough to begin on-street driving lessons.

Unit 1.1: Orientation
Introduces student to course content and vehicle through classroom lecture.
Instructor points out key components of tractor-trailer in demonstration.

Lesson 1: Orientation to Tractor-Trailer Driver Training, Classroom
Lesson 2: Introduction to the Tractor-Trailer, Classroom
Lesson 3: Orientation to the Tractor-Trailer, Lab

Unit 1.2: Control Systems
Introduces students to functions, operation, and meaning of instruments and controls, e.g., gear shift, tachometer, etc.
Instructor points out controls, instruments, and their operation during demonstration.

Lesson 1: Introduction to Vehicle Instruments and Controls, Classroom
Lesson 2: Instrument and Control Familiarization, Lab

Unit 1.3: Vehicle Inspection
Detailed classroom instruction on how to inspect tractor-trailers before operating, while in operation, and at the end of a trip.
Instructor will demonstrate pre-trip inspection.
Students will practice and continue practicing throughout course.

Lesson 1: Vehicle Inspection Procedures, Classroom
Lesson 2: Vehicle Inspection Practice, Lab

Unit 1.4: Basic Control
Students introduced to basic vehicle operation and concepts in class.
Instructor demonstrates starting, stopping, and backing with students.
Students take turns at controls of a tractor-trailer.
Students gain initial practice in basic control on range.

Lesson 1: Introduction to Basic Control Maneuvers, Classroom
Lesson 2: Starting and Turning off the Engine, Range
Lesson 3: Putting the Vehicle in Motion, Range

Lesson 4: Turning the Tractor-Trailer,
Range

Unit 1.5: Shifting
Students introduced to basic gear shifting procedures and shift patterns for most common
tractor transmissions.
Instructor demonstrates shifting on range.
Students practice shifting up through the first
three gears.

Lesson 1: Shifting Procedures, Classroom
Lesson 2: Development of Shifting Skills,
Range

Unit 1.6: Backing
Students introduced in classroom to methods and
concepts of backing a tractor-trailer.
Instructor demonstrates and students practice
variety of backing exercises on range.

Lesson 1: Backing Procedures, Classroom
Lesson 2: Development of Backing Skills,
Range

Unit 1.7: Coupling and Uncoupling
Students introduced to procedures for safely coupling and uncoupling a tractor-trailer.
Instructor demonstrates coupling and uncoupling
procedures and students begin practice under
supervised conditions.
Students develop proficiency throughout course
by performing activity before and after street
session.

Lesson 1: Coupling and Uncoupling
Procedures, Classroom
Lesson 2: Coupling and Uncoupling Skills,
Range

Unit 1.8: Proficiency Development: Basic Control
All skills learned in units 1.2–1.6 practiced.
A series of basic exercises are practiced on the
range until students develop sufficient proficiency to drive on the street.
Initial on-street practice occurs after sufficient
proficiency is developed on range.

Lesson 1: Introduction to Proficiency
Development Exercises, Classroom
Lesson 2: Proficiency Development Exercises,
Range
Lesson 3: Proficiency Development, Practice
in Basic Control, Street

Unit 1.9: Special Rigs
Handling and operational characteristics of vehicles on which students are not trained (e.g.,
tankers, refrigerated vehicles) are discussed in
class.
Field trip taken to observe special rigs and special
rigs observed during all on-street practice.

Lesson 1: Characteristics of Special Rigs,
Classroom
Lesson 2: Observation of Special Rigs, Lab

Section 2—Safe Operating Practices

Purpose
To allow students to learn and practice safe operation techniques in highway traffic.

Unit 2.1: Visual Search
Classroom instruction on the principles of visual
search.
Range instruction on the use of mirrors.
On-street practice in use of visual search
techniques.

Lesson 1: Visual Search Principles, Classroom
Lesson 2: Use of Mirrors, Lab
Lesson 3: Application of Visual Search, Street

Unit 2.2: Communication
Classroom instruction on communication, e.g., signaling, use of horn, etc.
On-street practice in communication techniques in variety of settings.

Lesson 1: Principles of Communication, Classroom
Lesson 2: Application of Communication, Street

Unit 2.3: Speed Management
Classroom instruction on speed management principles, e.g., maintaining safe speed in variety of situations, operating on hills, curves, etc.

Lesson 1: Speed Management Principles, Classroom
Lesson 2: Speed Management Demonstration, Range

Unit 2.4: Space Management
Classroom instruction on principles of managing space in traffic, e.g., following distances, space to the sides and rear, passing, etc.
On-street driving practice in space management techniques.

Lesson 1: Space Management Principles, Classroom
Lesson 2: Application of Space Management, Street

Unit 2.5: Night Operation
> Classroom instruction on inspection at night, preparation for night operation, hazards of night driving, and actual operations at night.
> Range practice inspecting vehicle at night.
> On-street lessons requiring application of night driving principles.
>> Lesson 1: Night Operation, Classroom
>> Lesson 2: Night Operation: Basic Maneuvers, Range
>> Lesson 3: Night Operation: On-Street, Street

Unit 2.6: Extreme Driving Conditions
> Classroom instruction on driving in cold and hot weather, stormy conditions, and mountainous terrains.
> Practice in putting on chains and towing a stuck vehicle.
>> Lesson 1: Operation During Extreme Driving Conditions, Classroom
>> Lesson 2: Techniques Used During Extreme Conditions, Range

Unit 2.7: Proficiency Development: Safe Operating Procedures
> All safe driving practices from units 2.1 through 2.5 (and unit 2.6 if applicable) practiced as students develop proficiency.
>> Lesson 1: Procedures for Safe Operation, Classroom
>> Lesson 2: Practice in Safe Operation, Street

Section 3—Advanced Operating Practices

Purpose
> To enable students to acquire the advanced skills needed to handle hazards and emergencies.

Unit 3.1: Hazard Perception
Classroom instruction and exercises in recognizing hazards early enough to prevent them from becoming emergencies.
On-street driving sessions involving application of hazard recognition principles.

Lesson 1: Recognizing Hazards, Classroom
Lesson 2: Application of Hazard Recognition, Street

Unit 3.2: Emergency Maneuvers
Classroom discussion of emergency braking techniques, evasive actions, and responses to other emergencies.
Emergency stopping and evasive actions practiced on range.

Lesson 1: Emergency Procedures, Classroom
Lesson 2: Emergency Skills, Range

Unit 3.3: Skid Control and Recovery
Classroom instruction on causes of skidding and jackknifing and techniques for avoiding and recovering from skids and jackknifes.
Student practice recovering from skids in skid pan exercises.

Lesson 1: Techniques of Skid Control and Recovery, Classroom
Lesson 2: Skid Control and Recovery Exercises, Range

Section 4—Vehicle Maintenance

Purpose
To prepare students to recognize causes of vehicle malfunctions and to perform simple maintenance and simple emergency repairs.

Unit 4.1: Vehicle Systems
Classroom instruction on function and operation of all key vehicle systems, e.g., engine, engine auxiliary systems, brakes, drive train, coupling systems, suspension, etc.
Instructor gives detailed description of each system, its importance to safe and efficient operation, and what is needed to keep system in good operating condition.

Lesson 1: Vehicle Systems, Classroom
Lesson 2: Vehicle Systems Demonstration, Lab

Unit 4.2: Preventive Maintenance and Servicing
Supervised student practice in vehicle servicing, including checking engine fluids, changing fuses, checking tire inflation, changing tires, draining air tanks and adjusting brakes, and performing emergency repairs.

Lesson 1: Nature and Importance of
Preventive Maintenance, Classroom
Lesson 2: Engine Fluids, Filters, Lights and
Fuses, Lab
Lesson 3: Changing Tires and Checking Tire
Air Pressure, Lab
Lesson 4: Reservoir Drainage and Brake
Adjustment, Lab

Unit 4.3: Diagnosing and Reporting Malfunctions
Classroom instruction on identification of vehicle malfunctions.
Students given a series of exercises in which they troubleshoot problems.
Students practice emergency starting procedures.

Lesson 1: Diagnosing and Reporting
Malfunctions, Classroom

Lesson 2: Emergency Starting Procedures,
Lab

Section 5—Nonvehicle Activities

Purpose
To enable students to carry out those activities not directly related to the vehicle that professional drivers must perform.

Unit 5.1: Handling Cargo
Basic principles of loading and unloading cargo, including weight distribution and techniques for securing and covering cargo.
Students practice loading a vehicle under instructor's supervision.
Students visit local freight handling company to observe operations.

Lesson 1: Basic Cargo Handling Procedures
and Requirements, Classroom
Lesson 2: Techniques for Loading, Securing,
and Unloading Cargo, Classroom
Lesson 3: Demonstration of Cargo
Securement, Lab
Lesson 4: Observation of Cargo Handling
Operations, Lab

Unit 5.2: Cargo Documentation
Discussion of basic forms and procedures required when driver handles cargo, e.g., bills of lading and other freight documentation.
Basic procedures and responsibilities for placarding vehicles that carry hazardous materials.

Lesson 1: Cargo Documentation: Basic Forms
and Procedures, Classroom
Lesson 2: Cargo Documentation Problems,
Classroom

Unit 5.3: Hours of Service Requirements
Classroom instruction in permissible hours of duty, rest periods, etc.
Introduction to and practice using driver log to record time.
Use of log to record time for remainder of course.

Lesson 1: Basic Requirements of Hours of Service Regulations, Classroom
Lesson 2: Complying with the Hours of Service Regulations, Classroom
Lesson 3: Log Keeping Exercise, Classroom

Unit 5.4: Accident Procedures
Basic instructions for handling the scene of an accident, reporting accidents, rules and regulations related to accidents.
Introduction to basic first aid practices.
Introduction to use of fire extinguishers and basic firefighting techniques, especially those related to truckers, e.g., tire fires.
Demonstration of use of fire extinguisher.

Lesson 1: Accidents and Accident Reporting, Classroom
Lesson 2: Principles of First Aid, Classroom
Lesson 3: Fires and Firefighting, Classroom
Lesson 4: Firefighting Demonstration, Classroom or Lab

Unit 5.5: Personal Health and Safety
Physical requirements for driving an interstate vehicle, medical examination, and certification.
Discussion of basic health maintenance requirements, diet, exercise, use of alcohol, drugs, and avoidance of fatigue.
Discussion of common nondriving safety hazards and use of special equipment, e.g., gloves, hard

hats, goggles, and equipment used with hazardous material.

Lesson 1: Personal Health and Driving, Classroom

Lesson 2: Safety Equipment and Practices, Classroom

Lesson 3: The Truck Driver's Environment, Classroom

Unit 5.6: Trip Planning

Class discussion of importance of and requirements for planning trips.

Federal and state requirements, including need for permits, vehicle size, and weight limitations, etc.

Classroom exercise in which students plan an overnight trip with school vehicle, including identification of permits, estimating time of arrival, fuel stops, etc.

Lesson 1: Trip Analysis and Trip Procedures, Classroom

Lesson 2: Trip Planning Exercise, Classroom

Unit 5.7: Public and Employer Relations

Classroom instruction and discussion on maintaining a good image, public relations problems of trucking industry, dealing with the public, and customers.

Classroom instruction and discussion of relationship to employer, including how to look for a job, get a job, and keep a job.

Student practice interviewing for a job.

Lesson 1: The Driver's Role in Public Relations, Classroom

Lesson 2: Employer Relations, Classroom

DIESEL AND HEAVY EQUIPMENT MECHANICS

The following is a curriculum of a sound course in diesel mechanics that should be taken by a young person interested in such a career. Your career or guidance counselor should be able to help you find a similar course of study in your area.

FIRST YEAR, FIRST SEMESTER	HOURS	CREDITS
Diesel and Heavy Equipment Power Plant	20	10
Applied Electricity-Diesel	4	2
Basic Communications	3	2
Applied Mathematics I	3	2

FIRST YEAR, SECOND SEMESTER	HOURS	CREDITS
Diesel and Heavy Equipment Chassis and Drive Systems	20	10
Related Machine Shop	5	3
Related Welding I	5	3

SECOND YEAR, FIRST SEMESTER	HOURS	CREDITS
Diesel and Heavy Equipment Electrical Systems and Carburetion	20	10
Metal Science	4	2
Applied Science	3	2
Applied Human Relations	4	2

SECOND YEAR, SECOND
  SEMESTER   HOURS   CREDITS

	HOURS	CREDITS
Business Practices	3	2
Applied Fluid Power	3	2
Diesel and Heavy Equipment Injection Systems and Hydraulics	20	10
Related Welding II	5	3

The Diesel and Heavy Equipment Mechanics program covers over-the-road and off-the-road equipment. Diesel and heavy equipment mechanics maintain and repair diesel engines that power trucks, buses, construction equipment, farm equipment, and industrial machinery. They perform preventive maintenance, follow troubleshooting procedures, rebuild components in repair shops, and respond to field service calls. They especially must be prepared to diagnose problems, make electrical repairs, and handle general welding duties.

Through classroom demonstrations and laboratory work, students study operating principles, repair processes, and rebuilding methods used to maintain gasoline and diesel engines and their supporting systems. The theories and physical skills necessary for proper disassembly and reassembly of various systems are covered. The fundamentals of the chassis and power train and the theory of operation are covered. The clutch, transmission, differential, hydraulic brakes, and air brake systems are covered in depth. Suspension systems and crawler undercarriages are studied. The program includes study of vehicle electricity, magnetism, and advanced electrical circuits and components. Testing and servicing of electrical systems are

emphasized. The theory, design, operation, and servicing of carburetion is included. Students study fuel injection systems and learn to service injection pumps, injectors, and nozzles. Hydraulics and fluid power are studied, with emphasis on diagnosis, repair procedures, and preventive maintenance.

Graduates of the program might seek employment as general mechanics or as specialists in fuel injections, engine rebuilding, transmission and drive train, brakes, crawler undercarriage, or electrical servicing.

DATA PROCESSING

The following is a curriculum of a sound course in data processing that should be taken by a young person interested in such a career. Your career or guidance counselor should be able to help you find a similar course of study in your area.

FIRST YEAR, FIRST SEMESTER	CREDITS
Business Mathematics	3
Introduction to Data Processing	3
Computer Operations I—Micro	3
Communication Skills I	3
American Institutions	3

FIRST YEAR, SECOND SEMESTER	CREDITS
Accounting I	4
Business Systems	3
Programming Logic and BASIC Language	3
Beginning COBOL Programming	3
Communications Skills II	3

SECOND YEAR, FIRST SEMESTER   CREDITS

Accounting II	4
Computer Operations II	3
COBOL II	3
Introduction to RPG Programming	3
Economics	3
Elective	3

SECOND YEAR, SECOND SEMESTER   CREDITS

Career Development	2
Small Data Systems	3
Advanced COBOL Programming	3
Computer Business Applications	3
Psychology of Human Relations	3
Elective	3

The use of computers in the processing of data has shown significant increases in recent years and is expected to display continued growth in the near and distant future. Businesses, large and small, depend on computers as vital sources of information. Today's technological world makes data processing a necessity for success. Computers offer opportunities and advancements that save time and increase productivity. They compute, evaluate, and store data for any kind of enterprise, affecting day-to-day and long-range operations. Computers provide business and industry with important financial and managerial assistance. They play a major role in dealing with inventories, accounting procedures, record-keeping operations, research, analysis, and other business matters.

Data processing requires skilled, knowledgeable, and capable individuals to operate, program, and supervise various computer systems. Potential sources of employment span a wide range of business and industrial organizations. Position opportunities might include systems designer, programmer, or operator.

The data processing program begins with basic computer concepts, including types of storage, input and output devices, general business use of data processing, and the physical operation of micro- and minicomputers.

Students learn programming by studying the internal functions of the computer. Basic flowcharting, logic, program documentation, and techniques for problem-solving are presented. The program offers various computer languages, including COBOL, BASIC, RPG II, and Assembler, as well as exploring software packages such as LOTUS 1-2-3 and BASE III. These languages are commonly used in business and industry data processing departments.

GENERAL OFFICE TRAINING

Many general office positions are available for those interested in a career in the trucking business. Those positions require various skill levels. While some of those skills may be obtained in a high school course of study, often an advanced business school course is desired. Listed here are two sample courses, a two-year Administrative Assistant/Secretarial program and a one-year Clerk/Typist program. Your career or guidance counselor should be able to help you find a course of study comparable to the samples.

ADMINISTRATIVE ASSISTANT/SECRETARIAL

FIRST YEAR, FIRST SEMESTER	CREDITS
Business Math Using Calculators	3
Shorthand I	5
Typewriting I or II	3
Communications Skills I	3
Psychology of Human Relations	3

FIRST YEAR, SECOND SEMESTER   CREDITS

Record Management	2
Shorthand II	4
Typewriting II or III	3
Communications Skills	3
Economics	3
American Institutions	3

SECOND YEAR, FIRST SEMESTER   CREDITS

Principles of Accounting	3
Shorthand III	4
Typewriting III or IV	3
Word Processing/Machines	3
Elective	3

SECOND YEAR, SECOND SEMESTER   CREDITS

Career Development	2
Shorthand IV	4
Administrative/Secretarial Procedures	4
Applied Data Processing	3
Elective	3

Administrators assume a wide range of tasks and responsibilities in the operation of most businesses and organizations. They must be skilled and flexible employees, ready to meet the varied and unexpected assignments of their employers. That means their duties extend beyond the major responsibilities of taking dictation, typing routine correspondence, and dealing with office visitors. They are often called upon to supervise the work of typists and clerical employees, compose correspondence, write reports, and do statistical research. They also must file, route mail, schedule appointments, answer telephone calls, keep minutes of meetings, and handle private or confidential records.

Because many offices are using computers, the students also work on dedicated word processors and perform business applications using microcomputers.

In the Administrative Assistant/Secretarial program, emphasis is on the development of shorthand and typing skills; these are among courses required during a student's first semester. However, a student who demonstrates proficiency through special testing may select advanced courses in these two skill areas. Progressive content in shorthand courses stresses shorthand principles, transcription rules, punctuation, spelling, and vocabulary in taking dictation of new material at maximum speeds. Emphasis is also placed on fast and accurate typing of business forms and letters, as well as special statistical records, accounting reports, and legal forms for executives and businesses.

CLERK/TYPIST

FIRST SEMESTER	HOURS	CREDITS
Clerical Record Keeping	5	3
Records Management	3	2
Business Mathematics Using		
Office Calculators	5	3
Typewriting I	5	3
Applied Data Processing	5	3
Applied Communications I	3	2

SECOND SEMESTER	HOURS	CREDITS
Office Clerical Lab	10	5
Typewriting II	5	3
Word Processing Concepts	5	3
Applied Communications II	3	2
Applied Human Relations	3	2
Career Development	2	1

The business office is the center of most organizations. Clerk/typist employees, responsible for a variety of assignments, are key members of the office staff. They continually deal with office communication operations, which include processing information, handling mail, and serving as receptionist. They must be ready to complete tasks manually and by machine.

The Clerk/Typist program is designed to prepare students for general clerical work and to allow them to specialize in one of several areas through the selection of appropriate electives. Typing is essential because practically all office forms, including letters, reports, and invoices, involve the use of a typewriter at some point in their preparation. Since many offices have word processing equipment, students receive hands-on experience with text-editing typewriters.

Overall records management procedures for sorting, filing, and retrieving information are also covered. Students are taught to operate various office machines, including text-editing machines, microcomputers, calculators, transcribers, and copiers. Telephone etiquette and visitor assistance are discussed. A basic course in record-keeping procedures (elementary bookkeeping) is included. Other necessary general clerical skills are also presented.

Graduates might seek employment in a number of clerical areas. Some possible positions include clerk/typist, general clerk, file clerk, mail clerk, accounting clerk, switchboard operator, receptionist, word processing correspondence specialist, and data entry clerk.

Appendix II

American Trucking Associations (ATA)
2200 Mill Road
Alexandria, VA 22314
(703) 838-1700
e-mail: trucking@edoc.com

Commercial Carrier Journal
201 King of Prussia Road
Radnor, PA 19089
(610) 964-4526
Web site: http://www.ccjmagazine.com

Professional Truck Driver Institute of America
  (PTDIA)
2200 Mill Road
Suite 600
Alexandria, VA 22314
(703) 838-1950

The following schools are certified by PTDIA:

ALASKA
Center for Employment Education
1049 Whitney Road
Anchorage, AK 99501
(907) 278-3674

Center for Employment Education
751 Old Rich Highway
Fairbanks, AK 99701
(907) 452-2959

CALIFORNIA
Advance School of Driving, Inc.
20825 Currier Road
P.O. Box 443
Walnut, CA 91789
(909) 595-2292

Truck Driving Academy
5168 North Blythe Avenue
Suite 102
Fresno, CA 93722
(209) 276-5708

Truck Driving Academy
5711 Florin-Perkins Road
Sacramento, CA 95828
(916) 381-2285

ILLINOIS
John Wood Community College
150 South 48th Street
Quincy, IL 62301
(217) 224-5362

IOWA
Transportation Institute of Des Moines Area
    Community College
5330 1/2 NE 22nd Street
Des Moines, IA 50313
(515) 262-1680

140

KANSAS
Fort Scott Community College
2108 South Horton
Fort Scott, KS 66701
(316) 223-2700

Fort Scott Community College
1401 Fairfax Trafficway
Building D, Room 355
Kansas City, KS 66115
(316) 223-2700

MICHIGAN
American Truck Driving School
150 South Michigan Avenue
Coldwater, MI 49036
(800) 999-8012

International Trucking School, Inc.
P.O. Box 811, Willowrun Airport
Ypsilanti, MI 48198
(313) 485-2700

MONTANA
SAGE Technical Services
3044 Hesper Road
Billings, MT 59102
(800) 545-4546
(406) 652-3030

NEBRASKA
Crete Carrier Corp.
400 NW 56th Street

Lincoln, NE 68528
(800) 998-9100

Northeast Community College
801 East Benjamin Avenue
P.O. Box 469
Norfolk, NE 68702-0469

NEW MEXICO
Albuquerque Technical/Vocational Institute
525 Buena Vista, SE
Albuquerque, NM 87106
(505) 224-3719

NEW YORK
Commercial Driver Training, Inc.
600 Patton Avenue
West Babylon, NY 11704
(516) 249-1330

OKLAHOMA
Ardmore Truck Driving School (ATDS)
P.O. Box 66
Gene Autry, OK 73436
(405) 389-5440

Oklahoma Vocational/Technical—Central
3 C.T. Circle
Drumright, OK 74030
(918) 352-2551

OREGON
Commercial Training Services

2416 North Marine Drive
Portland, OR 97217
(503) 285-7542

Pennsylvania
Highway Safety Center
Indiana University of Pennsylvania
Indiana, PA 15705
(412) 357-4051

Lebanon County Career School
18 East Weidman Street
Lebanon, PA 17046
(717) 274-8804
(717) 274-6036

Lehigh County Vocational/Technical School
(in partnership with SAGE Technical Services)
4500 Education Park Drive
Schnecksville, PA 18078-2599
(610) 799-1372

Texas
Career Education, Inc./ATDS
P.O. Box 41
Prairie Hill, TX 76678
(817) 344-2313

Utah
C. R. England & Sons, Inc.
4701 West 2100 South
Salt Lake City, UT 84120
(800) 453-8400

WISCONSIN
Fox Valley Technical College
1825 North Bluemound Drive
Appleton, WI 54913
(414) 735-5784

IN CANADA
Canadian Trucking Association
130 Slater Suite 1025
Ottawa, ON K1P 6E2
(613) 236-9426

Glossary

bid To offer a certain price; a payment or an acceptance.

commission A fee paid to an employee for performing a service or making a business transaction.

conscientious Performed with care to ensure that something is done correctly.

depersonalize To take away personality or human quality.

deregulation The government's removal of laws and rules from the trucking industry.

grievance A complaint filed by an employee because of a stressful problem, such as poor working conditions.

interdependent When companies and people rely on each other to get a job done.

lucrative Profitable; producing money.

overcapacity Surplus of something, such as products or services, in relation to public demand.

overhead Fixed cost of a company, such as insurance and rent.

prerequisite Something that is necessary to performing a function.

soliciting Trying to ask or get something.

tailgating Driving dangerously close behind another vehicle.

Teamsters union Union that represents truck drivers and dockworkers.

terminal Place where LTL carriers load, unload, and consolidate shipments.

workers' compensation System of insurance that reimburses a company for money paid to an employee who is hurt while on the job.

Index

.